THE CABBALISTS

AND OTHER ESSAYS

by

S. A. HIRSCH, Ph.D.

KENNIKAT PRESS
Port Washington, N. Y./London

THE CABBALISTS

First published in 1922
Reissued in 1970 by Kennikat Press
Library of Congress Catalog Card No: 74-102572
SBN 8046-0732-X

Manufactured by Taylor Publishing Company   Dallas, Texas

TO
THE MEMORY
OF
MY DEAR WIFE

PREFACE

THE essays in the present volume were composed at various times, mostly as lectures. It is difficult for me to say when they originated, as they are the results of life-long pondering on topics which obtruded themselves on my mind, in the same way as they have exercised the minds of many other reasoning men ; and I reproduce here the views to which an anxious and careful reflection has led me.

The first essay—on the Cabbalists—is the only one of the series that has seen the light before. It appeared, under the title of *Jewish Mystics—an Appreciation*, in 1907, in the October number of the *Jewish Quarterly Review*.

The *Prolegomena to a Philosophy of the Jewish Religion* are not exhaustive even as prolegomena. Many more questions besides those propounded would require close treatment. For instance, the great subject of *Ethnical Psychology*, which has such a far-reaching bearing upon the philosophy of the Jewish Religion, is here no more than just hinted at.

That subject is, however, incidentally alluded to in the following essay on *A Universal Religion*. The views expressed there met with considerable dissension among some of my friends. They would have preferred their own particular persuasion to be the goal for universal adoption. I must, however, abide by the convictions which my own considerations have forced upon me.

Another friend, for whose reasoning powers I have the greatest respect, asked me, whether the universal acknowledgment of one only God, which I put as the possible maximum for general adoption, was not a *big assumption*? Of course it is, so is religion itself, so is universal religion, so are innumerable other conceptions which have obtained the nature of convictions. They are demanded by the *Categorical Imperative* ; but some people of different mentality may perhaps reject them for all that. The same gentleman remarked that he found some parts of that essay very amusing. The passages he alluded to may amuse the reader, but I know the keen pain which they gave me when I penned them.

The incentive to write on the possibility of a Revelation, was a sentence of Mr. Claude Montefiore sufficiently indicated in the article itself.

The essays on *The Mishnah*, on *Rashi*, and on *Public Disputations in Spain*, explain themselves.

The last of the series, *Pfefferkorniana*, is complementary to essays on *Johann Reuchlin*, and on *Johann Pfefferkorn*, which are contained in my *Book of Essays*, which appeared in 1905.

I cannot conclude this preface without mentioning that the present volume might not have been issued at all but for the interest taken in its publication by my friend, Mr. Israel Zangwill. Mr. Zangwill took the matter in hand, and it is due to his energetic measures that I am enabled to offer it to the public. Needless to say that I am grateful to him, and I tender him herewith my sincere thanks.

S. A. H.

LONDON, 1922.

CONTENTS.

THE CABBALISTS

IT is to be hoped that the time has passed when the term "Jewish Cabbala" suggested the notion of a store-house of magic, black art, and witchcraft. It is no longer assumed by anybody to be a secret art of star-gazing, prognosticating, horoscoping, and soothsaying. Even such as have given only slight attention to the matter must have learned that there are many points of view from which the Cabbala may be considered, and that it may possibly have an interesting side even for the uninitiated.

It would be impossible to give even a cursory sketch of the Cabbala without diving down deeply into the intricacies of abstruse systems, without touching upon questions which require the most minute care of the specialist. A history of the Cabbala and its systems, of its various manifestations, applications, and influence, however exhaustively treated in detail, would, at most, elucidate one side of the question only. Another aspect would have to be investigated which would command a much higher interest. The purely human question would have to be entered into, and an attempt made to understand the workings of the intellect and the emotions, the interaction of religious thought and religious feeling, the wonderment at that which surpasses human intelligence and the craving to grasp its import, ethical principles and yearnings of the heart, which one and all are instrumental in calling forth the manifestations of man's mystical instincts.

But apart from such encyclopædic consideration of the subject, there are certain points which well bear to be dealt with exoterically. There are, on the very fringe of the subject, two questions capable of being investigated, without the necessity of entering upon abstruse reasoning and obscure details. There is, first, the question whether the term "The Rise of the Cabbala," frequently used in Jewish literature to denote the period commencing with the twelfth century, is not somewhat ill-chosen ; and, secondly, whether the judgment passed on the mediæval Cabbalists by several Jewish writers on Jewish history is not altogether erroneous.

Regarding the first point—the so-called rise of the Cabbala about the twelfth century—it must be said that it is no longer a dogma of modern Jewish historiography. Prof. L. Ginzberg, in his article on the Cabbala in the *Jewish Encyclopædia*, disposes of the notion that the Cabbala of the period alluded to was a newly risen star on the Jewish horizon. There is no abruptness in the genesis of the Cabbala of that time. It is a natural continuation of certain modes of thought and feeling which had never been absent; which, in one form or another, had all along prevailed in Judaism, and the actual rise of which may be said—from an historical point of view—to lose itself in the dim, distant regions of antiquity ; and—from a psychological point of view —to be rooted in the construction of that eternally inscrutable enigma which is called the human soul.

In reference to the second point: the way in which many Jewish scholars judge of Cabbalists and Cabbala, is one of condemnation only. The mystical element, which has played so important a part in the history of the Jewish religion, is anathematized. Mysticism, it is said, can only flourish in intellectual decay. Mysticism is represented as a poisonous plant of exotic origin, some seeds of which, having been wafted by an unfortunate wind upon Jewish soil, tended to cover large stretches of fertile regions with its outlandish parasitical growth. The Cabbala is described as an importation from without, an enemy of all intellectuality, of all rationalism. The lurid light which it professes to cast upon questions of the highest importance tends only to make the obscurity all the more palpable, so that the darkness can be felt. The Cabbala does not, indeed, hesitate to attack the most difficult problems in the arena of philosophy and metaphysics; but it tries to solve them, not by methodical reasoning, but by giving free license to unbounded imagination ; by inventing supernatural situations and combinations, which are based upon nothing, and obscure instead of enlighten; to degenerate ultimately into an inane juggling with numbers and with the letters of the alphabet. Stripped of all circumlocution it comes to this : that the Cabbala is said to be nothing but religious mania with a method; lunacy raised to the dignity of a science.

And as for the results which such extravagance leads to, they are deplored as having been pernicious in the highest degree. They are represented as having marred the Jewish conception of the Deity in its absolute spirituality; as having introduced a gross anthropomorphism ; an unsound idea of the soul and its duties ; and curious notions about life after death. This, it is said, led again to absurd rites to the detriment of the exercise of essential religious duties. The Cabbala, in short, is represented as having become, since the thirteenth Christian century until comparatively recent times, a bad sore upon the body Jewish, paralyzing it to a great extent, and endangering its very existence.

But it is not all scholars that judged thus harshly of this phenomenon in history. There are some who admit that the Cabbala has also its good sides, that some of its developments had a genuine spiritualizing effect. They concede that the flight of its imagination was in many cases highly poetical ; that its doctrines frequently conduced to intense religious devotion. But such gracious concessions do not go beyond admitting that an avowedly bad case has its redeeming points ; in accordance with the trite adage, that nothing is absolutely bad.

In the face of such absolute condemnation on the one hand, and a condescending semi-defence on the other, I claim for the Cabbala that the fact of its existence was a good thing, and not only a good thing but a necessity ; that it is a thing of which Jewish historians ought to speak with pride. I assert that the Jewish intellect could not have been of the high order which we would fain believe it to have been, that it must have been feeble indeed, if, in certain contingencies, it had not taken shelter in the Cabbala.

But I do not wish to be misunderstood. It is not my intention to break a lance either for or against the validity of the various doctrines of the Cabbala. I shall even grant—for the sake of argument—that such mysticism was foreign to the doctrines and objects of Judaism. Let it be admitted—for the sake of argument—that it was Neo-Platonism, and some other more ancient systems, the shoots of which were grafted upon Jewish beliefs and customs, and that every doctrine put forth by the Cabbalists rested on error. Yet, even so, I aver that a Jewish historian, taking up the standpoint of uncompromising antagonism to the Cabbala, and even whilst combating its tenets, would,

on the ground of historical justice, be obliged to
find that the fact that the Cabbala existed was an
aspect of the Jewish mind of which he, as a Jewish
historian, ought to be proud.

It is for this purpose that it may be useful to
receive some sidelights from the contemplation of
mediæval Christian mysticism. It will be profitable
for three reasons. First, there is some similarity
in the causes which prompted Christian and Jewish
minds alike to find solace in mysticism. In the
second place, the fact that mediæval Christian
mystics looked for inspiration into the books of the
Jewish Cabbala goes far to vindicate the significance
of the latter. There is a third reason which is not
so complimentary to us, and which issues from a
hope that Jewish writers may take an example from
the way in which Christian writers on the history of
philosophy treat their mystics. Nobody will suspect
these Christian scholars of having themselves an
inclination towards mysticism; and it is therefore
worth noticing, aye, and imitating, the historical
objectivity with which they assign to those mystics
their proper place in the development of human
thought.

Let us just enquire what the objects are which
mysticism tries to accomplish. For mysticism is
one of the instincts that enter into the composition
of the human being. It has its uses and its abuses.
It tries, in its own way, to find solutions to the host

of enigmas by which our existence is surrounded. The questions of why, whence, whither, how great, how long, are constantly before us. The horizon of mental vision is limited; questions crop up on every side. Must we silently acquiesce in the fact of our existence, and the existence of everything else—that is, if we and everything else exist at all, for this has also been doubted—without ever being able to understand whence everything took its origin, what it consists of, to what purpose it all tends, how this universe came into existence, what was its primary cause, how far it extends, how long it endures?

Of such questions there are two which mainly harass the mind : one, that of the genesis of the world, of the visible, palpable world ; and the second, that about its originator. The former question is partly put to us by our perception through the senses, and both by the workings of our mind. They already forced themselves upon the attention of primitive man. But the primitive mind was unable to conceive abstract ideas ; its ideas were conceived in a visible, material form ; it could not draw a line of demarcation between things material and things immaterial. The senses had to supply answers to the questions that vexed the mind. The forces of nature became the primitive man's gods. Every luminary in the sky, every tree, every brook and river, every breath of wind represented to

him, or was peopled by him with wonderful beings,
demons, gods.   And when he tried to conceive his
gods apart from the phenomena of nature, as beings
endowed with free movement, action, and volition,
his abstractions did not rise above the forms of men
and animals.   He may have exaggerated the size of
the members of the body and their powers, but he
would not carry his notions beyond those of colossal
men and monstrosities.   It was mythology which
attempted to satisfy in this way the cravings for a
penetration into the invisible.

A remarkable fact strikes us in connection with
this.   The same race which formulated mythological
fancies in the most attractive manner, the race whose
fabulous theogony and cosmogony appeals most to
the sense of poetry, that very same race, of all
ancient nations, has striven to free the intellect from
the trammels of fancy, and attempted to solve the
mysteries of existence by means of purely speculative philosophy.   The ancient Greeks, the masters
of the plastic representation of the Beautiful, who
possessed the most poetical system of mythology,
were also the first teachers of Logic and Metaphysics.   They produced their Hesiodic and
Homeric poems, and also their Socrates, their Plato,
their Aristotle.

I must not stop to investigate to what extent, even
among the ancient Greeks, imagination on the one
hand, and Orental influences on the other, formed

a link between crude mythology—crude, however poetical a garb it may wear—and purely philosophical inquiries. It suffices to notice these two methods, the mythological and the philosophical, by which it was attempted to penetrate the mists that envelop us.

But there was another way in which to answer the questions of the why, the wherefore, the whither, and the whence. Religion answered these questions in its own way. It did not limit itself to the requirements of the intellect and the imagination; it embraced besides the cravings of the heart which strives to come into closer connection with things divine. Europe, America, Australasia, and the greater part of Asia and Africa owes the most transcendental conceptions about God to the Israelite race; the conceptions of God as creator, as the only God, who is incorporeal, omnipotent, omniscient, of infinite mercy. Henceforth, no more worship of the phenomena of nature, of demons, of things material. An answer is found to the highest metaphysical problems, the yearnings of communing with God are gratified, and the prospect is held out of a universal acknowledgment of God by all mankind.

It would be an error to suppose that the relations between philosophy and religion were always of a hostile nature. They often were in opposition to each other; but, much more frequently, they lived together on terms of intimate good fellowship. They tried to supplement each other. Religion, or, rather, those who professed a certain religion, always liked to show that whatever religious doctrines and religious practices they adhered to, they were not merely a matter of pure faith, but the necessary outcome of certain primary principles. Philosophy of religion arose ; it set itself the laudable object of harmonizing, of reconciling, conflicting elements. The question whether a reconciliation was possible was not asked. The attempt was made, and, marvellous to record, it succeeded ; at least to the satisfaction of those who were willing to adopt its results.

Thus for ages man has been questioning and answering. Phenomena were explored, knowledge was piled up mountain high. Each generation added to the store ; the range of vision widened, the secrets of nature were laid bare. Knowledge enabled man to enslave the forces of nature and make them serviceable to the construction of gigantic undertakings. But all these acquisitions were accompanied by an undercurrent of insecurity. The questions of the where, the whither, the why, and the what remained unanswered. Some scientists and philosophers of the present age have endeavoured to take stock of our achievements towards the solution of these enigmas. They were constrained to admit the existence of limits to our knowledge which they despaired of man ever being able to traverse. The physiologist, Emil Du Bois-Reymond, concluded his lecture on *Die Grenzen der Natur-kenntniss* with the following words : " In respect to the riddle : What is matter and force, and how are they enabled to think, the explorer of nature has no choice but to adopt as his motto : *Ignorabimus.*" The same scholar gave, in 1880, a lecture at the Leibnitz-meeting of the Berlin *Akademie der Wissenschaften* before a gathering of scholars and scientists of the most advanced school. The lecture was entitled : *The Seven Riddles of the Universe.* The lecturer puts forward seven difficulties ; he concedes reluctantly and doubtfully the possibility of being overcome at some future date to only three of them, to wit : (1) the question about the origin of life; (2) the apparently intentional and tele-ological arrangement in nature; and (3) origin of thought, and—connected therewith—origin of speech. But he declares the other four difficulties to be insuperable; or, as he calls it, transcendent. They are : (1) the nature of matter and force ; (2) the origin of motion ; (3) the origin of simple perception through the senses ; and (4) free will ; in case we are not prepared to deny its existence altogether, but declare the subjective sense of freedom to be an illusion. The seven problems, he says, may be comprehended under one single problem, *the problem of the Universe* ; and this time he concludes with the motto : *dubitemus.*

This it is what modern research was candid enough to admit; and it is that which has been given voice to at all times. Religion, and particularly Jewish religion, told of the existence of a partition which it is impossible to penetrate. Thus, for instance, the Mishnah deprecates the attempt to understand the infinite space and time, saying that "he who ponders over the following four things might as well not have been born ! What is above, what is below, what is in front, and what is behind." But the human mind is like a child in leading strings. It is impatient of restraint. It refuses to acknowledge boundaries. It is surfeited with doubts, and thirsts for certainty. It is ashamed of asking and finding no answers. Thus Du Bois-Reymond's propositions were not allowed to pass unchallenged. He met with contradictions from many quarters; not the least important of his opponents was Ernst Haeckel, who attempted in his own way to give a solution of *The Riddle of the Universe.* But then, neither were Haeckel's conclusions allowed to pass unchallenged, and he himself found reason to modify certain of the results previously arrived at by him. The same old questions continue to be the subjects of meditation, and, when we glance at the literature which has sprung up, and revolves round them, in the comparatively short period of time that has elapsed since Du Bois-Reymond's pronouncement, we are bewildered by its extent.

But although religion was frequently satisfied with the acknowledgment of ignorance, and, as we have seen, some recent scientists and philosophers also, it was not the case with ancient, mediæval, and comparatively recent philosophy. It certainly was not the case with the mystics.

It is not surprising that philosophy did not satisfy the mystically inclined mind. It found one system of philosophy supplanting another. Besides, pure philosophy appealed only to the intellect. But can it ever satisfy the soul's craving for communion with the divine? Can it slake the yearnings for a sight of the invisible, for comprehension of that which is incomprehensible? The mystic is dissatisfied with the philosopher who invites him and his problems to his intellectual laboratory, but leaves his thirsting soul as parched as before.

Let me illustrate this by a phase in the history of modern philosophy. Immanuel Kant opened an epoch in philosophy which cannot be said to have come to a close yet. This philosopher started his meditations on the basis of the systems which preceded his. He found them insufficient; he rejected them one after another, and ended in—metaphorically speaking—constructing a great waste-paper basket, into which he unceremoniously bundled a number of previous philosophical tenets, after having torn them to rags and tatters. Fichte continued the work, and demolished the little that had been spared by Kant. But his follower, Schelling, went boldly forwards, discovered fresh insufficiencies, and ended by surrendering himself, hand and foot, to mysticism. The philosophical chrysalis had become metamorphosed into a mystical butterfly.

Such transition from philosophy to mysticism finds numerous counterparts in ancient and mediæval times. The causes are identical. The German philosopher, Eduard Zeller, expresses them in the following terms: " The mystical turn of mind revolts against a science which wants to define, to demonstrate, to discuss everything; which wants to invest the divine mysteries with human notions. And these notions themselves were too dry and too poor to meet the requirements of the mystic's profound nature, to give expression to the inspirations of his genial mind. The strictness of the logical forms oppressed his thinking powers; which were, indeed, bright enough to notice the contradictions of many distinctions, but were yet too much limited by religious interests and dogmatical traditions to remove the last causes of these contradictions. He took refuge in dictatorial sentences of pious consciousness ; in notions devoid of clearness, but ingenious and rich in fancies."

Such are the terms which a German philosopher applies to the mediæval German mystics ; they are the estimate by a Christian philosopher of the Christian mystics of his country. They are the words of an antagonist of mysticism, who maintains that such mystic speculations " cannot possibly have any lasting influence upon the conditions of knowledge, because they undertake to solve the most complicated and comprehensive questions by means of unclear notions and dogmatic propositions which have not been proved. Instead of well-defined ideas, they offer a confusing mass of fluctuating figures ; instead of scientific research, fanciful fictions ; instead of intelligible series of thoughts, apocalyptic riddles."

We see how outspoken Zeller is in his deprecation of mysticism as compared with pure philosophy. We must not stop to enquire whether the boundary line between mysticism and philosophy can in reality be so sharply defined ; whether "fanciful fictions" were not, more or less, important auxiliaries in the construction of both ancient and modern philosophical systems ; how much, for example, Leibnitz's monadology owed to a lively phantasy; how considerably Haeckel, when setting up his alleged solution of the Riddle of the Universe, drew upon his powerful imagination. It is enough for us to notice how so uncompromising an opponent of mysticism as Zeller does not look down with contempt upon the mystics of his country. Far from it; together with other historiographers of philosophy, he tries to dive down into the souls of these men, to understand their doctrines, and to assign to them their place in the pantheon of men of profound thought. There is no condescension here on his part; there is an honest attempt to discover in their endeavours an influence for the good; and he points to them with pride as members of the race to which he belonged.

Our Jewish mystics have not received such delicate handling at the hands of some of our modern Jewish writers. It would not be difficult to explain why the method of pitying condescension, or of merciless condemnation, or even supercilious ridicule, has been applied by Jews to Jewish mystics. I must, however, add that there were others who considered them from a much more reasonable point of view. Nor must it be forgotten that among Christians also the cases are by no means rare, that men who deserved the gratitude of contemporaries and posterity were not appreciated for the good they had attempted to accomplish, but lived in the memories of men as wizards and magicians, as, for example, Roger Bacon and Theophrastes Paracelsus.

The commencement of methodical mysticism loses itself in the fogs of ages. A real or supposed Pythagoras is said to have acquired some profound mystical doctrines when travelling in the East. Whoever Pythagoras may have been, or whether there ever was a Pythagoras, so much is certain, that there existed a Pythagorean school of philosophers. Pythagoras, or his school, considered the essence and principle of all things to consist in numbers ; numbers were the elements out of which the universe was constructed. All the various forms and phenomena of the world have numbers for their bases and their essence. On the foundation of numbers a cosmogony was constructed. Pythagoras was said to have been the first who taught the harmony of the Spheres, and the doctrine of the transmigration of the soul is also connected with his name.

We are just as ignorant as to the time when Jewish mysticism crystallized itself into a system. It may have originally been based on Chaldæan doctrines, but it was of a specifically Jewish character long before Christian mysticism had developed itself. The principal elements which the Jewish mystic had to blend together were reason, mystical promptings, and his Torah. This latter element, the Torah, served as a wholesome check to an untrammelled license in his speculations. If he was induced to adopt the priority of matter, his scriptural loyalty confined him to the priority of certain matter only. If God is to him the dwelling-place of the Universe, the Universe is not the dwelling-place of God. God, says Philo, is called המקום, the Place, because he enclosed the universe. He is himself not enclosed in anything. Mystical speculations continued to develop themselves for centuries before they led up to mediæval Cabbala. There were the ten Sefirot which were explained as the ten agencies through which God created the world: Wisdom, Insight, Cognition, Strength, Power, Inexorableness, Justice, Right. Love, and Mercy. There were notions about spirits and angels. There was the doctrine of the mysterious powers of the Hebrew alphabet. This mystical use of the letters of the alphabet bears an analogy to the Pythagorean method of explaining the universe through numbers. The book *Yetzira* plays an important part from the very earliest times. The letters of the alphabet were considered to resolve the contrast between the substance and the form of things.

Such doctrines, and many more, were further cultivated for centuries. They prevailed during the period of the Geonim. They existed in Babylon and in Italy, and from Italy they were carried to Germany. Jewish mysticism in Germany in the thirteenth century was not at all unlike the Jewish mysticism that prevailed in Babylon about the beginning of the ninth.

This is not in accord with those writers who aver that the Cabbala of the twelfth and thirteenth centuries was an entirely new departure in Judaism. It has been maintained that about that time the Cabbala arose as a new system of fantastic doctrines, that were invented by some mystics, and that this system succeeded in obtaining recognition among large numbers of Jews. It is said that it grew apace, that it assumed formidable dimensions, and finished by obscuring the horizon of the Jewish mind, and to replace clear notions by fantastic fabrications and puerile games with numbers and the letters of the alphabet.

I do not intend now either to endorse or to contradict these views, except on the one point, about the novelty of the departure.   The new Cabbala was nothing but a continuation and further development of the mysticism that prevailed at the time of the Geonim.   It is true that about that time the Cabbala derived additional authority from the belief that it was rooted in an antiquity of quite a different nature.   People believed that at the beginning of the twelfth century the doctrines of the Cabbala had been revealed by the prophet Elijah to Jacob Ha-Nazir ; that the latter had transmitted the new revelations to the great Rabbi Abraham ben David of Pasquières, whose son, Isaac the Blind, and the latter's alleged disciple Azriel, divulged them to larger circles.   We smile perhaps at the *naïveté* of those who earnestly believed in such stories.   But it requires a certain amount of *naïveté* of a different kind to assume that Isaac the Blind had been the inventor and originator of the mediæval speculative Cabbala.   It is much too complicated a work to owe its origin to the efforts of one man The works of Azriel contain traces which point to origins of a much earlier date.   Further investigations have shown, as I said before, that these doctrines existed in Babylon and Italy, and from Italy they were carried to Germany about the beginning of the tenth century. As to Isaac the Blind, we cannot say more than that he contributed largely to make the Cabbalistical tenets public property.

I shall not give a catalogue of names of those who were the bearers of the Cabbala of that period, nor of the books in which their doctrines had been laid down. Those who have given attention to the subject will have read about the book *Azilut*, the earliest book in which the speculative Cabbala is expounded. Its doctrines of the four graduated worlds, and of the concentration of the divine Being, and its angelology, are entirely based on the book *Yetzira*, and do not differ much from the view held on these matters by the Geonim. The author of the article Cabbala in the *Jewish Encyclopædia* says that it is probably a product of the Geonic period.

Another book in which the doctrines of the speculative Cabbala are fully expounded is the book *Bahir*. Its author is unknown ; but, as was the case with a number of Cabbalistical books, an author was found for it. It was ascribed to one of the Talmudical Sages. Probably the book had no author, but a compiler, who placed the doctrines that had been current in several schools of thought upon a dialectical basis. The book *Bahir* has the merit of having given to the Jewish scholars of the time an opening towards a thorough study of Metaphysics, which had, until then, been carried on only on the lines laid down by Aristotle. It is not necessary to give here a description of the book *Zohar*, and the opinions for and against it. The Spaniard Azriel (1160-1238) made the metaphysical aspects of the Cabbala accessible to the Jewish philosophers of his time. The notion was current at that time that we are only able to predicate of God that which he is not ; that all attributes of God cannot go any further than abrogate from him corporeal and material imperfections. This idea was followed up by Azriel. He starts from the negative attributes of God, and calls God the *En-sof*, the One without End, the One without Limitation, the absolutely infinite One, who can only be comprehended as the negation of all negations.

If we desire to gain an independent judgment about the value, the motive, and the effects of such speculations, the best method will be again to cast a glance upon similar phenomena in quite different spheres of thought. Let us see what Christian mediæval mysticism of that age, and of subsequent ages, had to say about them.

Towards the end of the thirteenth century the Dominican monk Master Eckhart proclaimed from the pulpit in the German language views which brought him into serious conflict with his ecclesiastical superiors. He had a thorough knowledge of Aristotle, Neo-Platonism, and the Scholasticism of his time. He had taught in Paris with great success. After visiting Rome he returned to Germany, and, for a number of years, taught and preached in Saxony, Bohemia, and Cologne. Proceedings were instituted against him, and he made a public recantation, but appealed, at the same time, to the Pope. He only escaped the papal condemnation by dying before it could take effect. The condemnation then fell upon his teaching.

Following previous doctrines, he distinguishes between God and the Godhead. God has a beginning and an end, but not the Godhead. God, or the Godhead, is exalted above all understanding; he has no existence; he is above every existence. He has no predicate; nothing can be attributed to him which could not with greater reason be denied of him : he is a non-God, a non-person, a non-form. He is everything, and nothing of everything. When dwelling in the nothing of nothing he is not God, but the Godhead, unpersonal, unbeknown to himself. In order to become known to himself it is necessary that there should be in him, together with existence, nature and form. Before things were created God was not God. He was obliged to communicate himself; God can do without creatures just as little as creatures can do without him. All things are equally in God and are God himself. Only nothingness distinguishes the things from God.

Compared with these and such-like enunciations of Eckhart's the obscure sayings of the Jewish mystics are bright daylight. People rightly consider Azriel's saying, the *En-Sof*, the absolute Infinite, can only be comprehended as the negation of all negations to be obscure. But how does it compare for obscurity with Master Eckhart's expositions? And we must not forget that Eckhart manages somehow or other to evolve out of his theory of God's self-conception, besides the revelation of God in a world, also the difference of persons in God, as the Christian Church teaches in the doctrine of the Trinity. It would be easy enough to declare the whole of Eckhart's mysticism to be senseless phantasy. But let us listen to the words of the great German writer on the history of philosophy, whom I had occasion to quote above, about that which, if it were written by a Jewish mystic, would have been stigmatized by many a Jewish writer as a farrago of nonsense.

"Scholasticism," Zeller says, "had forcibly united two incongruous elements; a faith which was under the guardianship of the ecclesiastical powers, and a science ruled by the tradition of the schools. Both elements had suffered by the unison. It had created a theology in which the sentiment of piety gained no satisfaction. . . . The Neo-Platonic idea of God in its original conception had removed the Deity to a distance, where it could not be reached by mortal beings; where, for itself, it would have no need of creatures; and the universe was brought forth by him only by the way, by an overflow of the divine power. Eckhart, on the contrary, was so much alive to the Christian idea of an intrinsic and real communion of man with God, that he was quite unable to conceive his God without universe and man. . . . This doctrine of Master Eckhart is certainly not a strictly philosophical system. It issues rather from religious motives than from scientific ones; and instead of an enquiry into reality which assumes nothing for granted, it starts partly from the Christian dogma, partly from previous speculations, especially Neo-Platonism. Yet has his doctrine, as compared with others, so much a character of its own, and it encounters the domineering system with so much boldness and independence, that we have every reason to see in it the first attempt of a German philosophy; the first vigorous flight of the German mind, which felt itself strong enough to think of emancipating itself from science, as it then existed, which was Romanic both in origin and substance; to excogitate a new form of research more in accordance with its genius and its wants."

I do not wish to use harsh terms about the views laid down in the books on Jewish history which deal with that which is called "the rise of the Cabbala." Those Jewish mystics who rejected the

Jewish mediæval scholasticism, which was called then, and is called still, Jewish philosophy, namely, the forcible harmonization of Aristotelianism and the Jewish faith, and welcomed instead the book *Bahir* and the doctrines of Azriel, these Jews may be glad if they meet with no worse epithets than haters of light and lovers of darkness. But the time will come when Jewish writers on Jewish mysticism will be animated by the same sentiments of impartiality, and true, scientific fairness as those which dictated the passages of the German philosopher which I have just quoted.

Systematic Christian mysticism in the later Middle Ages commenced with Eckhart, and its zenith was reached in the methods of Jacob Böhme, the cobbler of Görlitz. There was a series of mystics between them, and they occupy a conspicuous and by no means contemptible niche in the history of philosophy. The question might be asked, why such tender regard is paid to men whose doctrines no one is prepared to adopt ? The reason is this. It was recognised that it was a necessity in the graduated education of Europe that such mysticism should arise. Is it imaginable that it was possible for the human mind, the learned human mind, to loosen itself at a moment's notice from the insufficiency and inanity into which mediæval scholasticism had sunk, and with one swoop to arrive at sound methods in philosophy and science ?

Is it thinkable that learned Europe should go to sleep one night steeped in the conditions of science, as it was understood by the followers of an Albert the Great or a Thomas Aquinas, to rise the next morning as adepts in the methods of an Immanuel Kant or a Darwin ? It is not thus that revolutions in the dominions of learning and cognition take place. Mediæval scholasticism on the one hand, and the achievements of a Galileo and a Descartes on the other, are wide and far apart. Their bridging over is not a question of time ; it is a question of transition, of intermediary stages, of evolution. According to the natural construction of the human mind, mysticism was one of these stages, through which an effete scholasticism had to be metamorphosed into a methodical philosophy and study of nature. It was a psychological necessity that mysticism should form one of the links between dogmatic philosophy and an independent exploration of nature, of metaphysics, and of the human mind. These are not arbitrary *a priori* assumptions, posited for the purpose of explaining by their means real or imaginary facts. They are historical facts, which force themselves upon the attention of the observer.

This it is what the writers of the history of philosophy—may they ever so much have been opposed to mysticism—have seen ; this is the reason why they acknowledge the merits of those

Christian mystics, who were, in this manner, instrumental in paving the way for the development of science of the present day. This it is what our Jewish historians do not seem to have understood in regard to our own mystics. What then ought we to have preferred to this "rise of the Cabbala"? As little as it was possible for a Master Eckhart or a Jacob Böhme to be a Galileo or a Leibnitz, just as impossible was it for Isaac the Blind or Azriel to be a Hegel or a Herbert Spencer. The only alternative they had was, either to continue modelling and remodelling the old harmonizing methods of the age, which were then called philosophy, or to turn to mysticism, to the natural stepping-stone from a fruitless scholasticism to independent scientific research. And, in doing so, our Jewish mystics had a great advantage over their congeners. If it is true, as Huxley expresses it in connection with the progress of science, that " by a happy conjunction of circumstances the Jewish and the Arabian physicians and philosophers escaped many of the influences which, at that time, blighted natural knowledge in the Christian world," how much more true is it that the Jewish mystics were preserved from many a block, against which the other mystics could not help stumbling, by their written and traditional Torah, by the Midrashic and Geonic literature and its developments, upon which they were able to fall back.

The Cabbalists of this period were also influential in another way. They gave a direction to the Christian mystics. To some of these latter the Jewish Cabbala came as a revelation. They were no longer able to construe Christianity on the lines of a tottering Scholasticism. Whither were they to turn for that which they called rationalizing their dogmas? They discovered that by means of some modifications they might force the Cabbala into their service. A circumstance favoured them. Several books of the Cabbala went under the fictitious names of some ancient sages as their authors. Now there were in those days a comparatively large number of Jews that had turned Christians, and who, in their renegade zeal, were more popish than the pope. They wrote books against Jews and Judaism, and some occasionally tried their hands at the manufacture of Cabbalistical books, into which they smuggled some veiled representation of the Christian dogmas. The Christian mystics eagerly took hold of the Cabbala for their purposes.

Foremost among them was the Italian count Giovanni Pico della Mirandola. When quite young he had been a pupil of the Jewish scholar Elijah del Medigo of Candia. But this master could not satisfy his mystical propensities, because he belonged to that section of Jews that were hostile to the Cabbala. He turned to another master, Joachim

Allemano, Rabbi of Constantinople, who lived in Italy. Pico was determined to find proofs of Christianity in the Cabbala ; and what cannot be accomplished if one tries hard enough ? And in his case it was not so very hard after all. He did not so much enter into the metaphysical side of the Cabbala as into its formal methods. By transposing at will the letters of the Hebrew alphabet, and by a free use of their numerical values, he managed to produce results most convincing to himself.

It was the same with the German mystic Agrippa von Nettesheim, and with the celebrated Johann Reuchlin, to whom the Cabbala had come from Italy.

Heinrich Cornelius Agrippa von Nettesheim was born in Cologne in 1486. His career was "half scientific and half political, but always stormy." He was first a soldier and followed the armies of the Emperor Maximilian. He was knighted, studied law, medicine, and languages. As professor in Hebrew at Dôle, in France, he publicly expounded Reuchlin's work on *the Miraculous Word*. Then the monks persecuted him, and he came to London and lectured there. After many vicissitudes he thought he had at last settled down in Metz. But he had to leave that town for two reasons : first, because he had the audacity of opposing the common opinion that the holy Anna had had three husbands ; and, secondly, because he had dared to defend a woman that had been accused of sorcery. When Louisa of Savoy, the mother of Francis I, appointed him as her physician, she wanted him also to be her astrologer. He was shocked at the idea and indignantly refused; but at the very same moment he was engaged in setting a horoscope for the Constable of Bourbon, for whom he prophesied a brilliant victory over France. He was expelled, and there was quite a rush to receive him elsewhere. He received offers from two German princes, from the King of England, and from Margaret, the governess of the Netherlands. He accepted the latter's invitation, and but a short time after he terminated his chequered career at the age of forty-seven years. One of his books bears the title of *De nobilitate et praecellentia foeminei sexus declamatio (a dissertation on the nobility and excellency of the female sex)*. The reader may decide whether this was penned by the scientific side, or by the political side, or by the mystical side, or by the purely human side, in the character of this versatile man. The book has been translated into English; I believe, twice. But his chief work is that on the occult philosophy. Here he handled the letters of the Hebrew alphabet with unheard of freedom. The book is full of tables and schemes of transposition of letters; and in this manner he manages to prove whatever he wishes.

The celebrated Reuchlin was a man of unfathomably higher significance than Agrippa von Nettesheim. He also started his career with the study of the Cabbala. He approached a great Rabbi with the request to supply him with books on the Cabbala, but the Rabbi replied that no such books existed in his place; he moreover advised him to have nothing to do with mysticism. Reuchlin wrote two Cabbalistical books; the one entitled *De Arte Cabalistica*, and the other *De Verbo Mirifico*, the *Wonderful Word*. In the latter book he also gives free scope to an arbitrary transposition of letters, and inserts between the four letters of the tetragrammaton the letter *ש*, so as to obtain the name Jeshuah, a composite name, to which he ascribes all sorts of miraculous properties. Great as he was as a humanist, his contributions to philosophy were feeble; and he assisted in fertilizing the ground for the new sprouting up of modern science more by his humanism—the other powerful lever in the upheaval of modern thought and science—than by his mysticism. Mysticism, not less than humanism, paved the way for a new era of independent research in philosophy and the knowledge of nature. Thus we see in Theophrastes Paracelsus's life and endeavours—which Robert Browning wished to make intelligible to the English public in a remarkable poetical composition—a striking illustration of the transition from the old to the new methods along the paths of mysticism. There were Jacob Böhme, Nicholas Cusanus, Giordano Bruno, who was burnt at Rome, who gradually led up to the possibility of a pure philosophy, and of science based upon research and experiment.

Looking back upon our Jewish mystics of the twelfth and thirteenth centuries, I cannot help considering them of deserving a higher place in the history of philosophy than a Master Eckhart and a Jacob Böhme; they had certainly much loftier aspirations than such men as Agrippa von Nettesheim. In estimating these Cabbalists I abstained from discussing the claims of the mystical element in human nature to a voice in the consideration of the highest problems; I did not touch upon the question what part these mystical instincts play in the systems of our most advanced metaphysicians and physicists. I have placed myself upon the standpoint of those who are uncompromisingly antagonistic to mysticism. But I aver that from this very standpoint our Cabbalists have been unjustly treated by most of our modern Jewish writers. Much has been said about the dire influences which the Cabbala has exercised upon the development of Judaism. Even if we were—for the sake of argument—to admit the existence of these abuses, these could not neutralize the merits of those whom the inexorable order of nature forced into the channels of the Cabbala. And it is more than questionable whether the influences of the Cabbala were as pernicious as they are painted. Thus, I have heard people enlarge with great concern upon the immorality which the doctrine of the transmigration of the soul has in its train. I need only point to some of our Rabbis who held this doctrine ; for example, to the learned R. Isaiah Hurwitz, better known as the Sh'loh, who indeed attained as great a height of ethical and religious perfection as is ever vouchsafed to man to attain. I will quote a few sentences on this doctrine of the transmigration of the soul, written by an author of quite a different stamp ; who will say that such sentiments can possibly lead to immorality of any description?

"Why should it be impossible," says this author, "for every individual to have appeared more than once in this world? Is the hypothesis ridiculous for this reason only, because it is the oldest? Because the human intellect alighted upon it from the beginning, before it was distracted and weakened by the sophistry of the school? Why is it impossible for me to have once before taken here all those steps towards my perfection which can bring to men merely temporal punishments and rewards? Why should I not return as often as I am capable of receiving new knowledge, of achieving new capabilities? Do I take away with me after one appearance so much, that it would not be worth while to come again? Is this the reason? Or is

it because I forget that I have been here already?
How happy I to forget it ! A remembrance of my
previous conditions would permit me to make a bad
use of those in which I now move. And have I
then forgotten for ever that which I must forget for
the present ? Or is it because too much time
would be lost for me ? Lost, indeed ! What
time am I then obliged to lose ? Is not all eternity
mine ? "

What mystic may have said this ? What Cabbalist
may have spoken these words ? They are not the
words of any Cabbalist or mystic. They are the
words of no less a person than Gotthold Ephraim
Lessing, the great Lessing, the clear-headed critic,
the calmly reasoning philosopher. They are the
concluding sentences of his treatise on *Die Erzie-
hung des Menschengeschlechts* (*the Education of the
human race*). Disagree with Lessing if you will,
but you will not be able to say that he needed to be
ashamed of these sentiments.

I shall conclude with Lessing's words. I am
strongly of opinion that our Cabbalists have not
always been fairly treated by Jewish writers of the
present time. The whole subject requires an entire
overhauling. But about this we need not be concerned. Jewish historiography is a comparatively
recent growth. Time will assuredly show where
the truth lies. And if anything, surely history is
able to say : " Is not all eternity mine ? "

PROLEGOMENA TO A PHILOSOPHY
OF THE JEWISH RELIGION

A Lecture read before the Jews' College Union Society,
London, 1909

SOME months ago you honoured me by an invitation
to read before you a paper on "The Philosophical
Basis of Traditional Judaism." My sense of gratitude for the kindness thus shown me was neutralised
by the conviction that it was impossible for me to
grapple with a subject like this. The more I considered the subject the more I saw how unable I
was to deal with it. The words "Traditional
Judaism" made me pause at once. The expression
serves well enough in discussions about certain
aspects of Judaism, and on occasions when no
particular precision is demanded. But in a disquisition in which philosophical exactness of the
terms employed is of paramount importance, I did
not see what use I could possibly make of the term
"Traditional Judaism."

If the *raison d'être* of Judaism has to be established
on a philosophical basis, our meditations must needs
result into one Judaism only, and it is when we have
reached the end of our reflections that the question

arises whether any adjective has to be applied, and, if so, which it is to be.

In a strictly philosophical enquiry one might even go so far as to make the question about the right of Judaism to exist, the result, and not the starting point of the investigation. As for the adjective "Traditional," it is, in an enquiry on strict philosophical lines, one of the most unfortunate. In the first place, given the term "Judaism," the term "traditional" is already expressed. The distinction between Judaism based on Scripture alone, and Judaism based on the latter in connection with such tradition as are called "Tradition" *par excellence*, has lost all its significance. Written Law and oral Law do not denote such a partition as many people would fain draw between the two. Speaking of the present time, both scriptural and extra-scriptural behests and doctrines are traditional. There is certainly a class of people who avow their obligation of adopting scriptural whilst rejecting the other traditions. But the grounds on which they profess to be bound by the former are purely traditional. For certain reasons, based upon tradition, they consider it their duty to adopt *in toto* a document which is neither more nor less than a tradition put to writing at a certain early period fixed by tradition.

Besides, if we look into the manner in which such loyalty to a certain written tradition is upheld, in the face of a total abrogation of the other class of traditions, we shall find that it exists more in name than in reality. Those who adhere to the written document, to the exclusion of the other traditions, call the former in question in almost every sentence, test it by data derived from other sources, retain what they choose, and reject more or less reverently all that does not fit in with notions acquired from without. That distinction between Scripture and Tradition as a ground of divergence is philosophically unsound, and had, as a matter of fact, ceased to be of any practical value.

Again, in reference to a philosophical basis of "Judaism," the *a priori* assumption of such is already unphilosophical. The question could possibly be put in this way : "Has Judaism a philosophical basis," and "if so, where is it to be found ?" And in that case the former question should be put first. But the treatment of the whole question is fraught with so many difficulties, and is, at the same time, of so delicate a nature, that I despaired of doing anything even approaching justice to the subject ; and that within the compass of a lecture. But when I reflected upon the task set me, to speak, not only about a philosophical basis of Judaism, but about "the" philosophical basis, a philosophical basis with the definite adjective, the only genuine basis, the one exclusively correct on which the whole structure would prove to rest, I resolved to resign. It may not be complimentary to my courage, but I finally struck my sails before an adjective of three letters.

All I can do for the present is to make a few remarks on certain philosophical aspects of Judaism. I should like to remind you that I take the word "philosophy" here in its strictest sense. If it were only a question of moralising on some prominent points of Judaism, of setting forth their grandeur, of extolling certain views about questions connected with our religion over others, it would be tolerably easy, but it would have nothing in common with philosophy. To test the very foundations of our belief by the standard of philosophical investigation is a task requiring considerable powers. I can do no more now than to sketch a few outlines, to give headings of chapters within the boundaries of which such disquisition may possibly be carried on.

We should, however, have to go back very far before we were in a position to attack the subject itself. As the first chapter, I would suggest an enquiry whether a philosophical basis of Judaism can possibly be found—"philosophical" always to be taken in its severest sense. You first posit "Judaism," and look afterwards for a philosophical foundation, with the firm determination to find one. What connection can there be between philosophy, which should posit nothing, and derive everything from the simplest primary principles, and the adoption of such a complicated and fully equipped structure as the Jewish religion ?

Strip Judaism, and reduce it to a few simple principles, select from the fulness of that which Judaism offers some thirteen, or even some three principles, ignore by doing so the innumerable elements that render Judaism specifically Jewish, and then try to test the principles thus gained by a philosophical standard conceived *a priori*. But even in adopting such method you posit much too much. A further reflection may make us nervous about the possibility of an *a priori* philosophy of the Jewish religion. We might, quite unphiloso-phically, posit as the starting point some major, into which we should, quite unconsciously, put exactly as much as, and no more than, we should be desirous of deducing from it. We should convince ourselves that we had deduced the existence of God, Revelation, *our* Revelation, and consistently, the particulars connected with this Revelation from some primary, some natural principles; we should set up certain moral, social, and religious ideals, and perhaps some hygienic and economical considera-tions, and prove them to underlie a number of behests, warnings, doctrines, contained in that which our religion offers. We could prove all this to our own satisfaction and to the satisfaction of all who feel inclined to abide by our arguments, but our proofs would not go any further.

But, it may be argued, if we call in question the possibility of an *a priori* philosophy of the Jewish religion, what will be our position in reference to an *a priori* philosophy of religion, Jewish or otherwise ? In this respect I would ask you to consider that, strictly spoken, no philosophy of religion has ever been attempted. It was always the philosophy of a certain religion, of religion A, B, or C, or it was philosophy which considered religion in the course of its metaphysical reflections.

But then we may argue : if religion in a general sense is thus shown to form an important chapter of metaphysics, what hinders us to separate that chapter from the curriculum that establishes the sum total of metaphysical investigations, to consider it on its own merits, and then to see what use can be made of it for the purpose of philosophically considering our own religion ?

But you will agree that it would be hardly consistent with an *a priori* philosophical consideration to pick out arbitrarily one subject out of those which form — excuse the expression — the metaphysical stock in trade, and obediently adopt, without considering them, the principles from which the philosopher obtained his views on religion. Besides, you would not find it an easy task—you would find the questions relating to religion to be so inseparably intertwined with the general metaphysical questions, that you wouid not be able to distinguish a line of demarcation. You would have to study metaphysics, and you would then find yourself at the first link of a chain, which would occupy you considerably before you arrived at the goal which you wish to reach, namely, a philosophical basis of Judaism.

If you heroically undertook the task you would already have gained the heads of three chapters : (1) general metaphysical principles from which a philosophy of religion might be deduced; (2) the philosophy of religion resulting from these principles; and (3) the results thus acquired applied to the Jewish religion.

Having gained this much you have gained nothing. If I had to carry on an investigation like this I am afraid I should not get over the first chapter. For the question of *a priori* judgments, as it has exercised the minds of philosophers since Immanuel Kant, would arrest us at the very threshold. *Der Alles Zermalmende Kant*—Kant who pulverises everything—was the description given of that philosopher by Moses Mendelsohn. It is impossible to give here an outline of the results of Kant's meditations. With an enormous effort he tore up the foundations of numerous maxims which were considered from olden times the pillars on which the notions about God, the Universe, and ourselves rested. He commenced his clearing operations at a time when, in Germany, philosophy had reached a certain state of security. The philosophers were so self-satisfied with the so-called Leibnitz-Wolffian philosophy. The Deity had been construed cosmologically, ontologically, and teleologically. Wolff had described the soul in all its details. Philosophers had to do no more than to trim and keep in order the philosophical tenets gained in this way. Mendelsohn had observed a flaw in the ontological proof of the existence of God, and applied a plaster to it. "Teleology ran riot and vented itself in physico-theological reflections. Starting points from which to deduce theological convictions were derived from the phenomena of storms and earthquakes, the properties of stones and plants, the construction of the body, the life and technical instincts of particular animals." The philosopher Zeller, in pointing this out, gives a rather amusing list of essays on such subjects, which appeared under such titles as " Bronteotheology," "Sismotheology," "Litheotheology," "Phytotheology," " Insectotheology," "Melittotheology," "Acridotheology," "Ischyotheology," etc. "The conclusions to be drawn," says Zeller, "from the propositions of Leibnitz and Wolff were ready to hand in all their details. Their successors not being able to submit these propositions to renewed investigations, and to look for a new scientific basis, nothing remained to them but to limit themselves to sporadic supplements of the Leibnitz-Wolffian system, and to utilise the principles offered by the latter, partly for the explanation and partly for the practical treatment of particular disciplines."

Then Kant appeared with his critical philosophy. The Critique of Pure Reason swept away the whole fabric on which so many convictions rested, by scrutinising our possibilities of cognition. When the work began to be noticed a great number of controversies were raised. The most honest of the old school of philosophy proved to be Moses Mendelsohn. He at once felt and pronounced publicly that his part in philosophy was played out ; and although in his intercourse with friends he expressed the hope that, after all, Kant's critique would not be of great importance, he was candid enough to confess that he did not understand that work.

But Mendelsohn's hope was not fulfilled. The period of Kantian philosophy has, even now, not nearly reached its limits, and it will, it appears, be a long time before Kant's philosophy will reach the stage at which that of Leibnitz and Wolff had arrived at Kant's time.

Kant has proved the impossibility of Ontology although he still adhered to an *a priori* notion of " Das Ding an sich," the substratum, of which we are only able to follow up the phenomena ; the on, the noumenon, substance, matter, or whatever term may be applied to it. Fichte averred that it was only the Ego which posited the Non-Ego. " Das

Ding an Sich" disappears, although it occasionally crops up again in subsequent systems.

Briefly, the fact that Ontology is impossible forces itself upon our conviction. With the disappearance of Ontology, what becomes of all those metaphysical *a priori* judgments from which a philosophical foundation of religion was to be deduced? If it is impossible to demonstrate the nature, and even the existence, of matter, how should it be possible to demonstrate the nature and existence of God, soul, creation, revelation, and the number of notions connected therewith? How will it be possible to recognise either the purpose or the origin of anything, physical or metaphysical? We mentioned the theory of the Ego positing the Non-Ego, but how is it possible philosophically to recognise the Ego?

The course taken by modern science in the investigation of Nature does not tend to improve the interests of *a priori* demonstration. Teleology will have to share the fate of Ontology. The theories of natural selection, of the struggle for existence, will ill accord with the theory that the adaptation of every detail of creation to a certain purpose was the *raison d'être* of its existence. If the theories set up by Darwin, and followed up since his time, be made the basis of our reflections, the result will be further inroads in the most universally adopted notions. I fear me that our notions of Development and Progress will stand a poor chance. I think I can make this clearer by enunciating it in the form of paradoxes, as follows :—

1. Everything in nature shows development. The development in nature is stagnancy because it is only a regular transformation of certain fixed amounts.

2. The sum of progress is equal to the sum of deterioration.

3. Birth is death and death is birth.

4. Every development begins with life and ends with life, and has life in all its endless intermediate stages. Every development has death at the beginning of its chain and death at the end. Development has neither beginning nor end.

5. Nature creates unintermittingly. Nature shows no new creation.

6. Even the most seemingly lifeless thing teems with life—lives. In reality, the whole Universe is an inert mass.

7. Motive and finality are observed everywhere. Every phenomenon is without motive and without aim. By generalising more and more motives disappear entirely.

8. Order and regularity, both of shape and sequence, domineer in nature. Eliminate man, and the world is a chaos.

Contradictions of this kind force themselves upon the mind now as they did in pre-Kantian times.

Certain mystics and philosophers, both before and after Kant, solved them simply by the theory that in God are united all contradictions, by the theory of the harmony of contradictions. Philosophers who scout that notion often thought to have solved them by some philosophical formula. They enunciated the difficulty, which they then pronounced to be a rule.

A formula of a different kind : " I do not know," " I do not understand," although common enough to theologians, seems rather repulsive to philosophers. And yet this formula forces itself to the front more and more. The cognition of substance is being admitted to have narrowed as the knowledge of the phenomena of nature widened. Scientists and philosophers of the most advanced school have tried to solve the riddles, and their verdict as to the subjects which exercise our minds to the utmost; their verdict is in some cases *dubitemus*, we shall always doubt, and in some *ignorabimus*, we shall never know.[1]

Thus, the ground upon which to construct not only an *a priori* foundation of the Jewish religion, of religion pure and simple, but also any *a priori* metaphysical judgments, has been removed from under our feet. The question then arises how to proceed ? It might occur to some that absolute negation would be the logical outcome. But this is

[1] See p. 11.

fallacious. Non-existence has been proved as little as existence. We might then be led to fall into that state of mind which induced so many to adopt a middle course, namely, agnosticism. There are many people who profess neither to believe nor to disbelieve, neither to affirm nor deny. But on reflection we shall see that hardly anybody has succeeded in living up to that conviction, if it be true that it ever reached that stage; in theory he denies, in practice he affirms, or *vice versâ*. Thus it is and thus it must be, because the agnostic, like his fellow, is a human being. Reason forces us to reject, reason forces us to assume. Neither blind faith in arbitrarily assumed tenets, nor severe idealism, nor exclusive materialism, will succeed in satisfying the cravings and regulating the conduct of man. Blind faith would have to resort to persistent, and yet futile, attempts to kill doubt, to kill everything that is essentially human in nature. Idealism cannot have anything but theoretical significance. Materialism rigorously applied to man's intercourse with his fellow, with wife and child, is nothing else but an abstraction, and has no existence in fact. There is, therefore, nothing for it but to face the matter, to reckon with man as he is, to reckon with human nature.

The way has again been pointed out by Kant. His distinction between Pure Reason and Practical Reason gives the direction. A number of notions which we are unable to arrive at by Pure Reason we are compelled to adopt by Practical Reason. We assume them because we must, it is imperative that we should do so. Kant's arguments were followed up and modified by his successors : they constitute a rational basis on which to work. But we must be careful to pursue such work according to the methods applied to science in modern times.

There is a complete similarity of method in our times between philosophy and physical science. Formerly, physical science not less than philosophy tried to construe *a priori* the nature of matter. Modern science recognises only observation and experiment, and starts only from phenomena. This is also done, or, at least, ought to be done, by modern philosophy. It is idle to speculate on the nature of the Ego and the Non-Ego. We have to assume both, and to consider the way in which they affect each other. What concerns us at this moment is the question, in how far practical reason compels us to accept the notion of religion, and in how far religion is an essential requirement of the Ego. The first question affects certain things beyond us, which would have existence even if no human being existed ; the second is purely a question concerning ourselves. Here we have again the headings of two chapters : one on the necessity or otherwise of religion to man, and the second on religion. It will be convenient to consider the second point first, for it has been denied that religion is a necessity, or even an advantage to man.

It is not denied that man is by nature endowed with religious instincts; but some are of opinion that it is one of those instincts which are injurious, and interfere both with our intellectual and our ethical nature. They opine that the ethical education is the highest object to satisfy the transcendentality of man's nature, and that everything beyond is superstition. Now, the chapter alluded to would have to consider this; it would have to investigate whether the religious instinct of man, the craving to commune with a Deity, is an injurious, or, at least, a superfluous item, unnecessary and removable without injuring the system. I do not doubt but that the enquiry would lead us to maintain that the moral instinct forms one endowment, and the religious instinct another, quite separate, endowment of the soul, both being part and parcel of human existence. Granted this, that the religious cravings and aspirations are factors to be reckoned with, religion as such would be posited in consequence, not less than ethics, even if it were not already demanded by the fact that the existence of God, though not demonstrated by pure reason, was nevertheless forced upon us by practical reason.

We have already spoken about the futility of all efforts to explain the substance of Divine existence. From time immemorial philosophers have been at

E

pains to manufacture and remodel God after their own image, after their own nature. So many philosophers, so many Gods. The mind of man ranges along the course from rigid pantheism to inconceivable spirituality. Outside philosophy the human mind alighted upon strange conceptions about the Deity. Primitive generations were only able to conceive abstract ideas under the forms of things palpable and visible. The phenomena of nature were worshipped directly or indirectly in the forms of persons. A gross demonology, a crude worship of things material prevailed. But neither popular beliefs nor philosophical scrutiny has resulted into such a conception of God as to be satisfactory at the same time both to our religous cravings and the demands of our reason. It either led to meaningless and even immoral rites, or it left the heart cold and cravings for a communication with God unsatisfied. The investigation carried on in this chapter will therefore have to deal with the question as to where we are to find the guide to lead us safely through the labyrinth of notions about God, to rescue us from aberrations and to show us what it really is to which the demands of religion must lead us, over and above the recognised demands of our moral duties.

A fresh chapter will be required here for fixing the method to be adopted in order to arrive at an answer to the questions put in the previous chapter.

Only one method suggests itself, the one which is in use in all disciplines that admit of observation and experience. Induction first, deduction stepping in at the proper stage, in order to arrive at construction. Samson Raphael Hirsch wrote about seventy or eighty years ago that the method to be applied to investigations about the Torah was the same as that applied to inquiries about nature. " In nature," he says, "the phenomena are facts, and we are intent to spy out *a posteriori* the law of everyone and the connection of all. The proof of the truth, or rather, of the probability of our assumptions, is again nature itself, by the phenomena of which we have to test our assumptions, so as to reach the highest degree ever attainable, which is, to be able to say, everything is actually as if our assumptions were true ; or, in other words, the phenomena brought under our observation can be explained by our assumption. It is, therefore, our duty to gather all experience that can possibly be obtained about the phenomena which are the subject of our investigations, etc."

That which is said here about the Torah applies equally to religion. "The Torah," Hirsch says, " is a fact like Heaven and Earth." So is Religion in its general sense. As proved in a previous chapter, Religion is a necessity, a law of nature, a fact like Heaven and Earth. We have, therefore, to assume it as a phenomenon; we have to trace its particulars and the various modes in which it found expression.

From these we must generalise, and the verification of the results must again be looked for in these particulars and modes of expression themselves. Consequently, we shall have to consider what we know about religion, and which phenomena in the region of religion the history of mankind offers.

The question will, happily, be narrowed, so as to confine ourselves to a distinct field for our observations of the phenomena of religion. For whatever interest the crude notions of the lower forms of religion may have for the anthropologist or the psychologist, we shall be entitled to neglect them in our enquiry, or, at most, to consider them very briefly. We have the right to direct our attention at once to religion in its most transcendental conception.

The Greeks developed the conception of the beautiful in the highest degree. They gave it life in plastic representations, and in their poetry. At the same time they became the world's teachers in philosophy. They possessed an elaborate mythology, based originally on the deification of the forces of nature, and finding expression in certain rites and obscure, questionable mysteries. The Romans gave the world the science of jurisprudence, but as regards religion they did not rise above polytheistic notions about the gods. Conceptions of a purer kind obtained with some peoples in the far East, that is to say, in their purer manifestations, particularly in those taught by the Buddha ; but even in them it is always the gods, only they are of various degrees ; higher gods, with an idea of a highest god, with which men should strive ultimately to be united, or finally to cease to exist. The crude worship or modes of worship into which these conceptions degenerate may be neglected.[1]

In whatever form, and to whatever length the enquiry may be carried on as to the physiology—so to say—of religious beliefs, we shall ultimately have to come to the conclusion that mankind owes to the Jews the most transcendental conceptions of God and religion. If only keeping true to the method of observing phenomena before anything else, we shall find that religion as promulgated by the Jews, taught to discard the worship of nature, and ideas conceived under the form of natural phenomena. Judaism is, therefore, that pheno-menon in regard to religions to which the aforesaid method must be pre-eminently applied. Judaism fixed the notions about God as to incorporeality, in-visibility, omnipotence, omniscience, love, and infinite mercy ; it established God as Creator, Providence, and Eternal. It demanded recognition of Him, and of Him only, and it held forth the prospect that all earth would be full of the recog-nition of Him " as the water covers the sea." Our chapter would have to deal with these and similar

[1] A fuller enquiry into these topics would be highly important, but it is beyond the scope of this lecture.

considerations about God and religion, and with the question as to what sort of worship the Jewish religion demands of mankind at large.

This would raise another problem requiring a chapter of its own. The subjects of consideration would be, first, in how far the Jewish notions about God and His worship have taken hold of the Jewish race ; secondly, in how far the nations have modified them ; and thirdly, whether such modification is an improvement or a deterioration. Christians aver that it was Christianity that gave the Jewish notions their pure spirituality. It is an astounding assertion, but the philosopher must reckon with it, and must do so again by the light of observation of the phenomena. He will then find that Christianity turned backward from the transcendentality of the Jewish notions in two ways. First, it returned to some extent to the primitive pagan impulses of conceiving abstract ideas in forms offered by physical nature ; and secondly, instead of taking man out of himself and lifting him up to God, it again made man the centre from which the conception of God starts and to which it returns. In the latter respect it reckons, moreover, too much with the emotions, to the neglect of man's intellectual, physical, and social endowments. Very momentous considerations these, over which I regret being obliged to hurry, but which would make the present chapter the most delicate of the enquiry.

The next chapter would investigate the question how the Jewish nation acquired its transcendental notions about God and religion. Two answers suggest themselves : it was either by a development of general human instincts, which were particularly keen in the Jewish race, or it was by direct divine interference, by revelation. Darwin, at the close of his "Descent of Man," applies the laws of physical evolution to explain the acquisition by man of his ideas about God. That the religious consciousness of mankind grew and acquired a determined shape, either by gradual development, or as a result of evolution, is a maxim which has acquired the authority of a creed. But the philosopher must have the courage to test its validity. Is religion progressive ? The same question obtains in reference to ethics : is ethics progressive ? This latter question, although not the subject of our enquiry, is, however, very much akin to it, for it is Christianity that claims to have bestowed upon the human race a higher standard of morality than ever known before, and much beyond that which Judaism offered. Let us hear what Professor Huxley replied when that claim was put forward. He says,[1] "But there are a good many people who think that it is obvious that Christianity also inherited a good deal from Paganism, and from Judaism, and that if the Stoics and the Jews revoked their bequest the moral

[1] *Science and Morals,* *Collected Essays,* IX, p. 145.

property of Christianity would realise very little."
And in his essay on "Agnosticism and Christianity,"
he says,[1] "Again, all that is best in the ethics of the
modern world, in so far as it has not grown out of
Greek thought, or Barbarian manhood, is the direct
development of the ethics of old Israel. There is
no code of legislation, ancient or modern, at once
so just and so merciful, so tender to the weak and
the poor, as the Jewish Law." . . .

On the point of the progressive nature of ethics
or otherwise it will be convenient to quote T. H.
Buckle on the subject, as it will save the necessity
of again hinting—within the compass of a lecture—
at particularly Jewish ethics. He says : "To do
good to others, to sacrifice for their benefit your
own wishes, to love your neighbour as yourself, to
forgive your enemies, to restrain your passions, to
respect those who are set over you ; these and a
few others are the sole essentials of morals ; but
they have been known for thousands of years, and
not one jot or tittle has been added to them." Buckle
adds in his notes : "That the system of morals
propounded in the New Testament contained no
maxim which had not been previously enunciated,
and that some of the most beautiful passages in
the Apostolic writings are quotations from pagan
authors is well known to every scholar. . . . Sir John
Mackintosh was so struck by the stationary character

[1] *Collected Essays*, V, p. 315.

of moral principles, that he denies the possibility of their advance and boldly affirms that no further discoveries can be made in morals. . . . Morality admits no discoveries. More than three thousand years have elapsed since the composition of the Pentateuch, and let any man if he is able tell me in what important respect the rule of life has varied since that distant period. Let the Institutions of Menu be explored with the same view, we shall arrive at the same conclusion," etc. . . . Buckle further quotes Kant's words that "In der Moral-philosopie sind wir nicht weiter gekommen als die Alten." (We have made no advance on the Ancients in moral philosophy.) The present chapter should, therefore, have to consider whether the cases of our moral and of our religious consciousness are not on a par in this respect. Moses Mendelsohn denied the historical development of religious ideas. The point of discussion would be, whether the theory of evolution, if adopted, can be of value, except in the region of physical phenomena, whether religious truths admit of development any more than mathe-matical axioms, and whether human progress has any scope except by the accumulation of increased knowledge.

The question whether the human mind is so constructed that it was able by its own unaided efforts to approach near, even ever so near, but yet not quite to the Jewish conception of the Deity, to the acknowledgment of the absolute unity of God, is of subordinate importance. It requires a certain amount of intellectual reflection for nations to diminish the number of their gods, and, at last, to arrive at the acceptance of no more than a duality of gods; as, for instance, a god of light and a god of darkness, or a god and an anti-god. But the gulf gaping between the cognition of even so small a number as two and the absolute Jewish mono-theism is so enormous, which to clear would require such extraordinary mental capacities, that it would be astounding if any nation had ever been able to accomplish it. The difficulty would be the same if the distinction drawn by some critics between monolatry and monotheism had any substance in fact. The motives for the drawing of that distinction would also have to be laid bare in the same chapter.

Our inquiries would next lead us to consider the phenomena offered by the Jewish traditions, written or otherwise, which form the sources from which the religions of the present time are mainly derived, and we should have to discuss the way in which they affect us Jews in particular. Here is material for a number of chapters, but only the merest indications can be given here.

Let me say at once that the apologetic chapters should occupy a very small space indeed. Let us put our own house in order, and recognition will follow, or not, according to the greater or lesser freedom of mind possessed by those outside. Apology should only be resorted to where direct attacks have been made. But then we shall be asked: have we not seen already that the Jewish religion expects that the earth become full of the knowledge of God "as the waters cover the sea"?

This opens up the question of Israel's mission, of that which Israel is meant to accomplish. How then should Israel proceed? Three ways suggest themselves: (1) aggressive methods, (2) defensive warfare, and (3) a third method—which is the essentially Jewish one—the constant watching over the machinery devised to accomplish the work, so that it may effect the desired result in a natural, *i.e.*, in a divinely directed manner.

The problem of a universal unity of worship is closely connected with these reflections, and deserves a chapter of its own. I firmly believe that our investigations will result in the acceptance of the possibility of a universal recognition of the unity of God without, at the same time, a union of all mankind in the mode of giving it expression, and certainly without a universal worship. As long as human nature remains what the experience of thousands of years showed it to be, religions will differ, even if one leading principle were universally adopted. An Esperanto or Volapuk religion will be as little realisable as an esperanto or volapuk language. Experience has shown that the sublime ideal of a universal religion has been at the bottom of all religious persecutions.

As for ourselves, being Jews, and remaining Jews, what does this Judaism demand of us? Again keeping strictly to observation, we shall, in the chapter devoted to the consideration of our relations to God, find that the leading principle is the fulfilment of God's will. Bliss—or salvation, or beatitude —and perfection, cannot be motives, but, at most, only accessory consequences. The ideas of the good of our souls, the saving of the souls, even when raised to their highest conception, are not devoid of the notion of enjoyment and utilitarianism, tending again to centre everything in man. God demands, not that we should merely enjoy or suffer, but, above all, that we should serve Him. Our religion offers us the machinery by which to keep this constantly before our eyes; to school our actions, thoughts and feelings to the execution of that duty. Man, when left to himself, is prone to forget, to neglect, to fall into all sorts of aberrations; not only such as alienate man altogether from God, but such also as lead him astray in the very desire of worshipping Him.

One of these errors is the idea that we are able to know God and serve Him by abrogating our human nature, by crushing our material requirements, or by reducing them to a minimum. If we suffer ourselves to be persuaded by our intellect to use the latter for questioning the demands of our other psychical possessions and our material needs, we abuse our intellect just as much as it would be an abuse of our natural impulses, our feelings, emotions, desires, to allow them to domineer over our intellect or our body. Man is not altogether intellect, nor altogether feeling, nor altogether animal; he is a totality of forces, none of which should predominate at the cost of the others. All psychical or corporeal forces should combine to keep the balance. Again, not all men are equally organised, and aberrations are inevitable. A regulator is wanted to check him and propel him as the occasion requires. Such regulator is offered us by our religion.

Experience teaches us that no human interest is safeguarded, without some chosen few who have its requirements particularly at heart, and devote themselves entirely to its superintendence. In religion that class of persons are called priests, and the performance of certain rites, in which the devotional consciousness of those who profess that religion culminates, is exclusively assigned to them. In the family of mankind such priesthood was assigned to a whole nation of hereditary priests, selected for that purpose from their aptitude to these duties, called the Jews, who—wheels within wheels—have again a hereditary priesthood of their own. The Jews were established to form "a Kingdom of Priests and Holy People"; to be the bearers of religion and of the service of God. As priests they received a system of rites, not binding upon the lay nations, but necessary to them in their pontifical capacity.

This system regulates above all things the actions; it is a guide how to regulate life. The highest pitch of moral perfection is demanded by this system, to serve as a substratum on which to base the religious requirements. That religion does not consist in the mere teaching of a system, in the mere exhortation to act in a certain way, in a mere body of maxims to point out the road, and then let everyone shift for himself in his attempts to keep to them. The training method of the Jewish religion is different; it educates, which means it bends the association of ideas into a certain direction, which adverse influences may slacken but never entirely unbend, much less force into the opposite direction. The Jew has to practise that which is good, he has to perform actions which symbolise all that is good and pure, and has to perform them as behests of the divine will. By practising them he is being trained to understand that the thing he was told to be good was good in reality; and it gives him the impulse to undertake for himself other actions similar to them, and, therefore, equally good. In this way action and thought come to affect each other reciprocally. Constant practice gives a distinct direction to his ideas and to groups of ideas, and distinct groups of ideas entail distinct actions. His associations and groups of associations receive a distinct direction. A single good or bad action does not make a good or bad man. The question is which associations and groups of associations predominate. If they were directed from the first only to the good, a bad thought, and certainly a group of bad thoughts, will have great difficulty to overcome the predominant good associations, and the man trained in this way is a good man.

The Jewish Law is the educational medium for the Jew's service of God ; it protects him who observes it from the arbitrary predominance of the intellect over the other psychical forces ; from the attempts of crushing the wants of the body or rational thought, or the emotions of the heart. Everything harmonises—and therefore, whilst lifting man up to God, is, at the same time, so essentially adapted to human nature. This it is which has not been understood, and which has so frequently been ignored by Jews themselves at various periods of their history. This misapprehension cannot be better described than in the words of Francis Bacon. He says : "Prosperity is the blessing of the Old Testament, adversity is the blessing of the New ; which carrieth the greater benediction, and the clearer relation of God's favour. Yet even in the Old Testament, f you listen to David's harp you shall hear as many hearse-like airs as carols ; and the pencil of the Holy Ghost laboured more in describing the afflictions of Job than the felicitations of Solomon." . . . "Yet even." This "yet even " gives the clue. Whilst in the Jewish Religion God is so sublimely divine, and man never is asked to abrogate his human nature, other religions tend to dishumanise man and to humanise God.

This far I have only dealt with general aspects, without entering upon details. I cannot do more now than add a catalogue of topics which would require discussion in separate chapters.

Analogy with other nations. Similar customs of other nations. Similar creeds of other nations. Revelations and divine manifestations alleged to have been received by other nations. Such analogy, such similitude is unavoidable. a will be equal to a, but a will not be equal to $a + x$. The gross amount of universally human features will be a, the distinctive Jewish characteristics will be x. We shall have to investigate the x inherent in Judaism. Our a will be equal to the universal human a, but it is the divine spark which constitutes our x. In this way we shall find out what it is that makes our Judaism specifically Jewish. We shall always find that the leading idea is the fulfilment of God's will.

We should have to consider the documents in which the system is contained, the sources from which it emanates, its historical basis, the results which it has achieved both within and without. We must consider what Judaism reveals about God, the world, humanity, Israel. What it teaches about justice to other beings, about love in obedience to God ; about symbolical representations in words and actions, about the exaltation and consecration of our lives. Once a hypothesis is gained from generalisations, the details of our divine inheritance must be constantly scrutinised, either in verification or rejection thereof.

We shall find that the details of our Law are to be kept in obedience to God, that it lifts us up to Him, and is instrumental in causing us to fulfil His will. All other aspects, as, for instance, social, moral, hygienic aspects are, at most, only concomitant. The real purpose is always religious. Those behests which are universally human are Jewish only from having the service of God for their motive and sole object.

F

A UNIVERSAL RELIGION

Lecture read before the West End Jewish Literary Society, London, February, 1911

I INVITE you to cast with me a glance upon the good side of human nature. A glance, and no more. No more than a glance is possible. The good impulses of the human heart are too numerous and too many-sided to converge to the focus of human comprehension. He who has experienced the greatest number of its manifestations has only witnessed a few of its aspects ; the most optimistic, and the most experienced withal, can only survey a limited tract within its infinite domain. This may be as true of the bad side of human nature. Perhaps so. But it is to one or two of the latter's functions in the good direction that I ask you to give your attention for a moment.

The wish to make others share the happiness we enjoy is not the least of our good impulses. Invaluable is the desire to relieve others of care and sorrow, of suffering and despair. The instinct to find truth is one of the noblest endowments of the human soul. The subjugation of our carnal inclinations, so as to make them subservient to the demands of ethics and religion, is a glorious feature in man's existence. These, and many kindred propensities, would be enough to give man the exalted position he occupies in the world of living beings.

These superior qualities have amalgamated, they have combined and formed one homogeneous entity. They have become the dominant power in man, in groups of men, in communities, in races. All the members of a people have consented to give that growth the fullest play, so that it might strike root, and from its ramifications, which would shelter all mankind, shower its blissful fruit over all, and bring it within the reach of every one. They set to work shoulder to shoulder, they engaged actively in the work of making the whole human race one mass of happiness ; and cries of anguish rose to heaven from all parts, human blood flowed like water, unheard of tortures were inflicted, wholesale massacres were instituted, wars of extermination supervened, the holiest bonds were dissolved, the human heart became brutalised ; for benefactors of mankind had resolved to befriend all the members of the human race, and to cause them to participate in the highest good attainable by man.

For these benefactors were convinced that they had reached the pinnacle of all that is desirable. They had persuaded themselves that the highest good did not consist in worldly possessions, in honour, in gratified ambition, in glory, in indulgence in the desires of the flesh. Their minds soared higher. They sought for that which was above themselves. They recognized that they depended on powers that were beyond their control. The religious instincts, innate in every one, asserted themselves. But they asserted themselves in different ways. Peoples acknowledged God, or acknowledged gods, each in his own way. The modes of worship differed widely, rites and ceremonies varied. The notions about a divine power, or about divine powers, found expression in various acts of worship.

Allow me to sketch briefly one of these developments, those of the Christian religion. Acts of religious worship came to be considered by many as inferior manifestations of man's conceptions of the divine, who, they thought, ought to be concerned about the conceptions themselves only. They placed the whole weight of man's duty towards God in the acknowledgment of these conceptions. They assumed that, once acknowledge these conceptions, you have absolved all your religious duties. Philosophical, or rather, theosophical speculations, had come to express that which was required to be acknowledged under the term of "the Word."

It was preached that in the beginning was the Word, and the Word was with God, and the Word was God. No one could be sure that he who acknowledged all those notions which were attached to that term "the Word" was really convinced of them in his heart.   But, at least, let him pronounce "the Word," let him assert his belief in "the Word," let him utter the formula, *i.e.*, let him acknowledge the notions which the term was assumed to express, and he was considered to have done his duty.

Again, a utilitarian motive stepped in.   The conception of a life after death became an inherent factor in the mental life of mankind.   It took various forms.   Suffice it for the present to note that form according to which the soul is believed to survive after the decomposition of the bodily remains. The soul is believed to be answerable after death for the lifelong merits or aberrations of its bearer during his lifetime on earth.   After death the soul is to be rewarded for the virtues or to expiate the sins of its bearer ; the soul is to enjoy the sweets of heavenly glory or to be condemned for ever, or for a long duration of time. The soul may be saved from perdition for all eternities by God's mercy.   But such mercy could only be vouchsafed by an intermediary agency, and then only provided that agency had been acknowledged.   Consider what interest of paramount importance was thus at stake.   It was either bliss and beatitude for aye and ever, or perdition and inconceivable sufferings, perhaps for aye and ever. Once convinced of the efficacy in this direction of the acknowledgment of "the Word" and the agency, and who would hesitate to pronounce it? Whose heart would be so callous as to withhold from others that healing remedy that bears salvation in its train?

Again, this desire of benefiting others, by that which was believed to be the practical result of religious duty fulfilled, gathered strength from another powerful motive. The belief gained ground that the service of God, according to the rites and actions of a limited community, of a race of men, was objectionable. It was erroneously assumed that such service of a particular body of men was tantamount to a disregard of the religious interest of all those who stood outside that body. Whatever the rights of the matter may be, a conviction spread that there could not exist religious duties in which all members of the human race were not equally bound to share. The duty of one was the duty of all. No attention should be paid to diversity of history and vicissitudes of race, of differences of psychological endowments between one group of men and another. It was thought that the religious beliefs, which people had persuaded themselves to be the only true ones, should be carried far and wide, so that every single member of every variety of the human race should be made cognizant of them. The duty was conceived of carrying the message, which was called the good message, all over the world. Only acknowledge the truth of the message, pronounce your adherence to "the Word," and then—you may hear the adage every day if you choose—and "then you are saved," by which they mean to imply that your soul, which was otherwise lost, would now be saved from perdition. The idea of carrying the message was taken up with an earnestness and a thoroughness which can only display itself in a cause of that kind. The message itself became subject to different interpretations, each of which claimed to be the sole true one. There was to be a catholicity of religious belief; the universality of religious belief which each of the representatives of the message considered the exclusively admissible one, was to be not only a universality in theory but a universality in fact. The motive power may have had its origin in some of the noblest impulses; the impulse to save one's fellow men from the most heinous of sins, to induce him to attain the highest virtue; to save him from eternal perdition, and instead, procure for him the means of securing eternal bliss and beatitude. The representatives of the good message carried, each his own interpretation, far and wide, and again the bearers of each interpretation strove to convert the bearers of all others to their own views.

They tried to achieve all this by sermons, by curses, by minatory ebullitions, by cold steel, by fire and water, by refinement of cruelty and torture, by wholesale massacres, by holocausts of communities of human beings at one time, by sanguinary wars of thirty years', or even eighty years' duration, by training craftiness, which is one of the lowest instincts, in such a way as to make it reach the highest summit of perfection, to go hand in hand with such unscrupulous cruelty as that introduced by Torquemada, by such organizations as the one founded by Ignatius Loyola, or by such sorry devices as to practise upon the innocent minds of young children, or to offer a cup of tea at a tea meeting, or a bottle of medicine, as tendered by the Bishop of London ; and, horror of horrors, by systematic missionarising.

Of course, we must not blind our eyes to the fact that it was not for long, that the disinterested motives and purely philanthropical impulses were solely at work to bring about these deplorable results. They were soon mingled with other incentives. When men are penetrated with the certainty that they hold the truth, they cannot but consider such as deny their tenets a menace to the foundations on which their own convictions rest. It is a blow to their self-approbation, which is more than their flesh and blood can bear, and which they cannot help resenting with all resources at their command.

Again, more selfish impulses soon learned how to make use of the noble idea of a universality of religion for their own gratification. Political aspirations found it a powerful weapon for the furtherance of their own interests. Ambition in the form of hierarchical domination found it a godsend. It proved a mighty instrument at the service of colonising enterprises, of the conquest and occupation of newly discovered territories, of the satisfaction of earth-hunger, that besetting sin from which many powerful states are suffering. The mischievous effects of religious missions abroad, in connection either with the furtherance or the disturbance of political interests, have never been so convincingly set forth as by so great an authority as the late Marquis of Salisbury, whilst he was Prime Minister of England. On June 19th, 1900, the Society for the Propagation of the Gospel in Foreign Parts met in Exeter Hall to celebrate the bi-centenary of their existence. It is noteworthy to observe how, on that occasion, Lord Salisbury would have liked to express his whole hearted approval of the work of the Society, but how his political conscience constrained him to utter some warnings which must have sounded very discordant to his audience. In the course of his remarks he said: " I am here perhaps rather a stranger, for I must not conceal from you that at the Foreign Office missionaries are not popular, and that perhaps the Foreign Office may look upon me rather as a deserter in appearing upon your platform at the present time. . . . But, as your president has pointed out, the means of communication were not (in former times) as they are now. . . . Now things are considerably altered, and that very increased means of communication, that very augmentation of the power of opinion and men to affect men by the mere conquests we have achieved in the material domain—those very conquests, while undoubtedly they are, as the Archbishop said, an invitation from Providence to take advantage of the means of spreading the Gospel, are also the means by which the lives of many and the acts of many which are not wholly consistent with the ideal which is preached in the pulpit, and which we read of in the holy book, are brought home to the knowledge of the millions whom we seek to address. . . . If an evangelist or an apostle, a Boniface or a Columba, preached in the Middle Ages, he faced the difficulties and underwent the martyrdom, he braved the torments to which he was exposed. . . . But now, if a Boniface or a Columba is exposed to this martyrdom, the result is an appeal to a Consul for the mission of a gunboat . . . it gives men the opportunity and the temptation to attach a different meaning to that preaching, and to suspect it of objects which are far away from the thoughts of those who urge it. They have a proverb in the East: First the Missionary, then the Consul, then the General." Speaking of the attempts to convert the Mahommedans, Lord Salisbury proceeded: "You will not convert them— I will not say you will never do so. God knows that

that is far from our fears. But, dealing with events of the moment, I think that your chances of conversion, as proved by our experience, are infinitely small compared to the danger of creating great perils and producing serious convulsions, and, may be, of causing bloodshed, which will be a serious and permanent obstacle to that Christian religion which we desire above all to preach."

But among these accessory motives, such as statecraft and priestcraft, the idea of a universal religion, though obscured, is not lost sight of. And it may be enunciated as an aphorism, that the idea of a universal religion is at the bottom of all religious persecutions. This is the more curious, because those very abuses would disappear of themselves should the ideal be realized, and because the abolition of those abuses is one of the main objects which the promoters of a catholicity of religion seek to procure. For, cut the knot, make an end of all diversity of religion and introduce universality, all religious hatred will die of its own accord. And therefore let there be a universal religion and catholicity of worship.

But at the very outset a difficulty obtrudes itself which it is impossible to surmount. What form of belief and worship is it that is to embrace the whole of the human race, that is to become catholic? Within Christianity only, there is Roman Catholicism, Greek or Orthodox Catholicism, Anglican

Catholicism, and several other denominations who believe that their form of faith is to conquer the world. Islamism professes to be the religion to the adoption of which all mankind should be compelled, even by force of arms. Kuenen took for the subject of his Hibbert Lectures, in 1882, "National Religions and Universal Religions," and it is obvious, even from the plural form of the title, that the word "universal" is not taken in the sense which the idealistic benefactors of mankind attach to it.

But I called the difficulty in the way of the realization of the ideal insurmountable. It is true, it is hoped to establish a catholicity of religion without the aid of an inquisition, without torture, without auto-da-fe's, without kidnapping of children, without test acts, without civil disabilities, or forced sermons, or pales of settlement, without spiritualising cups of tea, or salvation bearing boxes of pills. The ideal is to conquer the world by means which would be worthy of the noble promptings that created it, stripped of all those paraphernalia which are, after all, only an abuse of exalted aspirations. Man is to be elevated to the highest conception of things divine ; all diversity in the region of religion is to disappear.

But which is to be that religion which is to succeed in bringing all members of the human race under its sole sway ? Where is the Moses who will promulgate this new and all-comprehensive creed, which will establish a religious brotherhood of all men, that will appeal to the religious instincts of every one ?

The question is whether those who are zealous for the establishment of such heavenly days upon earth have reckoned with human nature. Can it be possible that any creed, or set of creeds, or any mode of divine worship, should appeal with equal force to all men in every quarter of the globe ? The idea may be conceived as possible, but this, I think, is as far as it can go. I do not think that it can ever reach the stage of actual existence.

Two factors are being neglected : first, the infinite diversity prevailing in the nature of man, and, secondly, the intrinsic diversity in the psychological constitution of such aggregates of men as have become communities, races, peoples. Too much is built upon the circumstance that after all we are all members of the same species. The theory that all men are or should be alike before the law of the land, leads to the idea that all are equally amenable to certain tenets which some people consider to be the truth ; that the variations observable between men and men touch only the outer forms of the species, but that the souls of men are alike in their nature, that the diversities are only influenced by accidents of soil, climate, surroundings, and circumstances, but that the souls, being intrinsically one

and all of the same nature, can be kneaded and
moulded to recognize truth and particularly, *the*
Truth *par excellence*. People who hold such
opinions do not for a moment stop to enquire
whether the varieties exhibited by men are not of a
more intense essence also in regard to their psychological endowments. They do not consider the
possibility that the differences noticeable between
men and men in different local centres, and in
different groupings, not only as regards colour,
build, and anatomy, but also in regard to intellectuality, sympathies, and propensities, may be the
results of what is called the law of nature ; the
causes of which are as much an enigma as the
causes of variation in the animal and vegetable
world. They do not even take note of the various
mental endowments between man and man within
the same domain, and consider the frictions conse-
quent upon them as accidental and easy of
adjustment.

How then could people who hold such views take
into account the characteristic differences that obtain
between whole groups of individuals ; the constant
variety they display in respect to intellectuality,
aspirations, achievements, ambitions, sympathies,
predilections ? They will not be able to acknowledge, not only that the souls of individuals offer
varieties which are innate and constant, but they
will stand aghast at the notion of constant varieties

existing in the souls of nations—I do not use the word in a mystical sense—which no intercourse and blending, no artificial assimilation, will be able to efface. Yet, distinctions of such type undoubtedly exist. Just as varieties of type within the same species of plants and animals occupy a distinct place in the economy of nature, in the same way characteristic distinctions in the psychological endowments of the different races of men occupy a place in the economy of the human race at large and a comparatively modern branch of philosophy *Völker-psychologie*, ethnical psychology, the psychology of races, attempts to discern the phenomena that present themselves. Indeed, it were irrational to say that variety was a law of nature. Nature is variety itself. In the beginning God created variety In the beginning God created harmony. Variety is a divine institution, and unity is nothing but the harmony of varieties This is the case with nature as a whole, it is also the case with the innumerable items of which nature consists. In every item, however minute, there is a variety of varieties. The variety may offer itself to our powers of observation the causes of such variation are withheld from our sight. A child can distinguish a grape from an apple, a grain of wheat from one of millet, vegetable substance from animal substance. A child can, but a scientist cannot; for the scientist dives down into the past history of each substance; and the deeper he dives the more he is confronted by chemical and embryonic identity, and the divergence in the nature of the substances as their history proceeds ; a divergence constant and irresistible, which he is unable to account for.

Thus, each member of nature's household is a mystery, and man is the mystery of mysteries. The whole family of men belong physically to one and the same species ; this is probably the case also in regard to his psychological nature. Yet are the varieties that characterise the different groups of humanity much more numerous than those that distinguish them physically. Moreover, the former are more difficult to efface, if it be possible at all. Let us only look round and notice the differences between men and men, even within the narrowest circles, as, for instance, those of learning, of commerce, of officialdom, differences which are not generated by outer circumstances, but are intrinsically peculiar to each individual.

But the differences that subsist between different aggregates of men are as pronounced, as stubborn, if not more so than those subsisting between individuals. The physical varieties among plants and animals, even of those that are closely allied, have long been recognised and described ; so have those of men. But not much has been done to fix the psychological divergences between groups of men that have formed themselves into aggregate bodies

of communities, races, peoples. I do not allude to
such differences as are generated by accidents of
circumstances and environment, and which disappear with the removal of their causes. I speak of
such variations as form an indissoluble link that
keep a body of men together, and also keep it apart
from other similar bodies of men that are yet so
dissimilar. Hence arise innumerable frictions, and
it is here that the blessed effects of harmony step in
and promote unity. The greatest blessing of mankind in their social and political intercourse is
nothing but the realisation of unity by means of the
harmony of varieties. The term friendship implies
it, the term brotherhood implies it, the term love
implies it. Separateness is a divine institution, and
over the multitude of separate existences that defy
amalgamation hovers the spirit of God, divine
harmony, and forms them into a unity. This
harmony between the endless modes of separate
powers has been so beautifully expressed by the
metaphor of the wolf and the lamb that are at some
future time to crouch peaceably together. Greed
will no longer be satisfied at the cost of innocence,
the weakling will no longer be haunted by the fear
of the violent. The ideal of harmony between
opposing, and even conflicting motives, is pictured
by the peace between the wolf and the lamb, but
not by the picture of a cross-breed between wolf
and lamb, which would be neither wolf nor lamb,

but an unnatural compound which might drag on its existence for a time but would be unable to propagate its kind.

Is it, therefore, idle to hope that the ideal of a universal religion will ever be realised ? Must we renounce the hope that a time will come when all men will be one in acknowledging the truth divine ? We involuntarily turn to some of the existing religions. The Jewish religion, which has outlived ages, has withstood so many untoward storms, and, at the same time, stamped other more recent religions with some of its typical characteristics, does not aspire after adoption by all mankind. Strange, for this it has been called a religion of separatism, of particularism ; whilst that religion which insists that its blessings can only benefit those who adopt it to the exclusion of all others is said to be universal ! There are other religions which have taken hold of vast multitudes, such as have been called by Kuenen universal religions. None of these will ever become universal in the sense which the term really implies. Nor will a hybridisation of a number of typical features culled from the various existing forms of belief and worship be otherwise than sterile, without possessing any lasting vitality. I may leave out of consideration the hopes of those who hold the highest accomplishment of man's ethical nature to be tantamount to the final demands of religion. The most sublime behests of ethics were known to several races in the remotest times; it is only their cultivation that has fluctuated; at some time, in some lands, they enjoyed obedience in great measure, at others they were more or less neglected or trodden under foot. But our ethical instincts and our religious requirements are two distinct factors, the one of which cannot possibly satisfy the innate cravings of both. The ideal of a universal religion would therefore have to presuppose that those who deny this, who are convinced of the all-sufficiency of ethical perfection, would renounce their views in its favour. Again, we should have to assume that all those to whom evolution is the one and all of every existence, that the agnostic, that the class of philosophers to whom all notions of things divine are declared to be phases of superstition, would all be brought within the fold of the universally professed religion. Will it ever come to pass?

After all that has been said the outlook seems gloomy enough. We can only look upon man as we find him, we can only reckon with the man of the future by the light of the man of history and of the present time. And yet we need not despair. We need not discard the ideal of a universal religion as a dream that lacks nothing except the possibility of realisation. The religious cravings of man have before them a vista of universal gratification. We may firmly hope, aye, confidently expect, the universal acknowledgment of the one sublime religious truth, a universal acknowledgment of God. But we must not extend our expectations beyond the confines of human nature. That religion will be universal only in as far as it will be the one and sole pervading motive. God, one God, absolutely one, without any admixture or association, will be the issue from which all religious persuasion will start, and to which all religious persuasion will return. When, as the prophet expresses it, "All earth shall be full of the knowledge of God, as the water covers the bed of sea," the boldest aspirations towards a universal religion shall have been realised. With this consummation the limit will have been reached. Then a universal religion will have been established.

But there will be no universality of worship. I have already sketched forth the grounds upon which I hold such universality to be impossible. Nor is it necessary. Not that our conception of that which is necessary or unnecessary would alter the facts which nature offers us. But it is possible that nature might have shaped man differently if that which is unattainable to us in our present state would constitute a necessity. But even as we are, with all the peculiarities of our nature, which, to my mind, make a universal mode of manifestation of the universally acknowledged truth an impossibility, the ideal, with all its limitations, is worthy of our loftiest aspiration. The knowledge of God by all men, whom everyone will serve, to whom every mouth will pray, before whom every knee will bend, in submission to whose rule and sovereignty the extremities of the earth will unite, is no small consummation of the ideal of universality of religion, and which the much lauded humanity of the present day is far from having accomplished. It foreshadows an ideal realisation of the sway of harmony among the diversified expressions of the universal religious truth, a cessation of the disastrous results which to this very day mar the elevating influences which the gratification of our religious instincts should exercise. A brotherhood of all varieties of man in the worship of God, acknowledged by all. A universal religion without the limitations that are marked out by the diversified characters that distinguish such various aggregates of men as form clearly defined groups. It will be the fulfilment of that prophetic prediction, that the time will come when all earth will be full of the knowledge of God as the water covers the bed of the sea. That promise, which, as I heard it once homiletically expounded, chooses advisedly the figure of the sea and its bed. The bed of the sea offers endless variation, the nature of its soil differs infinitely, its surface is uneven, with its mountains and hills, its valleys and its ravines ; the sea which harbours a fauna and a flora, the numerous diversities of which dazzle the imagination. But all this

multiformity is covered by the water of the sea
which unites it, and constitutes the element in which
it exists, and changes, and lives, and flourishes, and
by which it is levelled, even in the way in which
the religious spirit of man will find its level, and
will live and thrive under the pinnacle of the
harmonisation of human diversity, the knowledge
of God.

I have in this lecture kept aloof from the theological aspects of the question. I have not touched
upon such points as revelation or any other
theological doctrine or belief. Nor have I taken
note of any specifically Jewish characteristics, of
Messianic hopes; topics which might shed a flood
of light upon the subject. I have not alluded to
that which stamps the Jewish religion as a well
defined phenomenon among the manifestations of
the soul as moulded within the unity of a distinct
aggregate of men. No repudiation will ever be able
to extinguish that religion so that its place in the
economy of racial human nature will know it no
more; and a hybridisation between some of its
parts and portions taken from other ethical and
religious varieties will never form a homogeneous
whole; it may live for a time, but is, if only by
virtue of its hybrid character, foredoomed to sterility.
I have compressed within the compass of a lecture
some general reflections to elucidate a subject, the
consideration of which should fill a book. Yet am

I convinced that the longer I were to study it, the more I should become confirmed in the views which I have endeavoured to lay this evening before you.

POSSIBILITY OR IMPOSSIBILITY
OF A DIVINE REVELATION

THERE is a little fortress, seemingly of small importance, garrisoned by soldiers who have apparently made no progress in the ar of warfare, sticklers to their antiquated weapons of defence, incapable of taking the offensive. It is positively believed that the fall of the fortress is only a question of time ; before long it will be stormed, the defensive works razed to the ground, and its existence become no more than an historical reminiscence.

The fortress has been assailed from the day of its foundation, ancient weapons of attack have been replaced by new inventions, instruments of supposed power of destruction have been employed. The garrison itself contained numbers of soldiers who were dismayed at the strength of the opposing forces, some even attempted to persuade their fellows to give up the struggle. But the bulk were staunch. Sorties were rarely made, the old defensive form of warfare was adhered to, and—wonderful to relate—the fortress still holds out, and defies the new weapons of precision, the tempered steel, the destructive explosives. The homogeneity subsisting between fortress, warfare, and garrison asserts itself. They form a front from which all hostile missiles rebound.

Our Jewish religion is such a fortress. It exists and will exist, in spite of all attacks from without and from within. It endures by force of its intrinsic strength ; by the necessity of its existence ; by force of its character, through which it is solely and exclusively adapted to its bearers ; it endures because it is one of those facts in the order of things which it is impossible to expel from its place in the economy of nature.

Do not ask me for a definition of the term "Jewish Religion." I mean the Jewish religion as it has existed since its initiation in hoary antiquity ; as it has manifested itself during a continuous succession of ages. Rooted in the Book of Books, borne upon the shoulders of tradition, the inheritance of a distinct people, overspread with the glamour of a holy country, nurtured by the instruction of God-enlightened seers, upheld by the teachings of self-denying sages ; it has promulgated to the world the unity of God in its absolute oneness, indicated the way towards the purest morality, moulded its bearers into a kingdom of priests, caused them to think it, to feel it, to live it, to perform its pontifical rites day and night, in houses and garments, in food and drink, in matrimonial and family life. It impregnated its bearers with loyalty to the demands of a glorious and inglorious history, of rejoicings and sufferings, which latter have surpassed everything that has been undergone by any compact body of men ; that Jewish religion which has outlasted the attacks levelled against every one of its aspects.

I do not allude for the moment to that class of opposition which has attempted to do away with that religion by means of crushing out of existence those who profess it, either by brutal force, or by coaxing prospects, or by wily kindness. I rather refer to the blows aimed against its doctrines, against the foundations upon which it rests, upon the mode of life in which it results. Argument followed argument purporting to invalidate the warrant for its existence, either in regard to the whole or some of its parts. Every age has contributed its share, every phase of human thought has helped in forging weapons of attack, every fresh acquisition of knowledge has been imagined to supply additional strength to the offensive.

It need not be said that the defensive has tried to ward off the blows. Some vigorous attempts have been made to meet the attacks against every single tenet of the Jewish religion. The apologetic literature is considerable. The defenders either endeavoured to invalidate the hostile arguments, or they employed a conciliatory method, and tried to weld together opposing forms of thought, often without inquiring whether a conciliation was possible; or, again, it took the more legitimate form of vindication, and engaged in investigating that which the Jewish religion offers, bringing it to the light, and allowing it to be its own spokesman.

The Jewish religion has survived, but its survival is not a result of such apologies; at most it has survived along with them. Its actual apology it bears within itself; if it had not within itself the necessity of its existence, no apologetic acumen would be able to prop it up. It lives because it is a distinct factor in nature's household, because it supplies, in a way peculiarly its own, some of the loftier requisites of human existence, because its followers hold a place of their own among the families of mankind. To know it is to vindicate it. Some of the apologies labour under two serious defects. First, as already alluded to, they frequently tried to reconcile the irreconcilable, to harmonise discord. Secondly, they attempted too much, they thought to be able to annihilate all and every argument at one fell swoop. No one person can combine within himself all the powers requisite to meet the objections drawn from most divergent regions of thought and knowledge. The highest dialectical skill will not avail against objections based upon historical considerations, nor will intimate acquaintance with text or language succeed against judgments derived from physical science.

For the defence to be effective a patient scrutiny of every single argument is required ; and the apologist, convinced of the justice of his cause— and only such are worthy of note—should abstain from approaching a second point before he has considered the first to the best of his abilities. It is only by a patient sapping and mining that he can hope to demolish the works of the besiegers.

I invite you, therefore, to consider with me for the present only one point out of the many that have been raised against our form of belief, and that only in one direction. It is the question whether a direct divine revelation is possible. I do not propose to investigate the question from its theological or historical aspects, but only to deal with it on purely philosophical considerations. I shall formulate the case in three sentences, as enunciated by Mr. Claude Montefiore, in a pamphlet issued by him in October, 1909. Speaking for himself and others, he stated as follows : " Our conception of God is not, I fancy, wholly the same as the conception of Him formed by the traditionalists. God does not, and, we may even venture to say cannot, reveal himself to man in the absolute way in which the orthodox conception implies. The idea that God speaks out loud human words, that He spoke to Moses what we read in the Pentateuch as a man may speak to his fellow—this idea has become impossible to us."

Before proceeding with the subject I wish to make a remark or two. When persons declare that a certain idea has become impossible to them, then, as far as they are concerned, nothing further is to be said. Secondly, I do not know, nor do I ask, whether Mr. Montefiore intended to convey in these words exactly what I understand them to mean. It is quite unnecessary, since it is not my intention to controvert Mr. Montefiore personally. My object is to controvert an idea, a conception, which I consider to be tersely and clearly enunciated in the sentences quoted. I see here a direct divine revelation disputed on account of its impossibility, and I wish to confine myself exclusively to that one point. I do not approach the question of evidence, of proofs that such a revelation has actually taken place. Nor would it be logical to do so. Once assume the impossibility of a direct revelation, the question of evidence for its actual occurrence becomes a quibble; for how can one assert that to have taken place which is impossible?

It is posited that " God does not reveal Himself in the absolute way which the orthodox conception conveys." More than that : " God cannot do so. How can God have spoken loud human words, how can He have spoken to Moses as a man may speak to his fellow " ?

The argument appears on the face of it plausible

enough ; but plausibility must never determine us, for plausibility is the arch-enemy of truth. On considering it, however, it seems difficult to meet. The conception of the Deity transcends everything human. We conceive Him as absolutely incorporeal. His being is devoid of all, the sum total of which constitutes man. Speaking, as we understand it, is a function effected by the human organs of speech, the mouth, the tongue, the vocal chords ; none of these instruments can be attributed to God in the same sense. Hearing is the function of another set of human organs ; the greater or lesser loudness of the words ; the very cause of hearing is understood to depend upon certain vibrations of the air, as it comes into contact, through the ear, with a certain set of nerves. Would it not be blasphemous to say that God produced articulated sounds with mouth and tongue and vocal chords, by means of which he caused the air surrounding Mosès and the Israelites to vibrate in such a manner as to make their ears hear His voice ?

There is no seeing without eyes, no speaking without mouth, no hearing without ears. Loud spoken words serve to convey the ideas of one person to another by means of these instruments. This we experience, this we understand. How can we then assume the possibility of the same effects being produced by that Being to whom the possession of such organs cannot be attributed?

Are not these reflections sufficient to declare a direct revelation by God to be impossible ? Are we not faced by the following alternative : either we must attribute to God organs of communication similar to those we have, or the possibility of such communication must be denied ?

But the question is, may there not be means of communication by spoken words other than those which have come within the precincts of our experience ? Would this be the assumption of an impossibility ?

It is the custom to declare all that to be impossible which does not accord with such conceptions of causes and effects as come under our experience. This is because the question of possibility and impossibility is confused with the problem of evidence of actual occurrence. We witness facts and incidents, and see them display a series of causes and effects, and we conclude that this is the only one possible. We are in the habit of calling any conception of things and events which cannot be explained by the canon established by our experience the conception of an impossibility. We argue, that for a succession of ages nothing has come under our cognisance except the existing proceedings. These we understand; we comprehend the causes that bring about the effects we witness. Then we are prone to draw the conclusion that only the operations occasioned by the agencies which we, and those before us, have witnessed, are possible; whilst that which we cannot explain by the same code of cause and effect is impossible.

But such reasoning rests on a misapprehension. It is a lack of discrimination between evidence and possibility. When asking what then can we call possible, we should be guided by the rule set up by David Hume. He says, "Whatever is intelligible, and can be distinctly conceived, implies no contradiction, and can never be proved false by any demonstrative argument or abstract reasoniug *a priori*." Professor Huxley gave his entire assent to this proposition. In the manifold controversies which this fighting scientist constantly carried on against all religious and theological traditions, either Jewish or Christian, he always took his standpoint upon the question of evidence, never upon that of possibility. In one of his essays, entitled "Possibilities and Impossibilities," he says: "Strictly speaking, I am unaware of any thing that has a right to the title of an 'Impossibility' except a contradiction in terms. There are impossibilities logical, but none natural. A 'round square,' a 'present past,' 'two parallel lines that intersect,' are impossibilities, because the ideas denoted by the predicates, *round*, *present*, *intersect*, are contradictory of the ideas denoted by the subjects, *square*, *past*, *parallel*."

1. Hume, "Doubts Concerning Operations of Understanding.," Part II.

H

Now, the conception that there is a living Being which differs substantially from anything living that has come under our experience, and that this Being is possessed of modes of communication with men, by which ideas are brought to the latter's consciousness, similar to the way in which man's spoken words awaken consciousness in his fellow, is intelligible and can be distinctly conceived. Therefore it cannot be proved impossible. The saying that God spoke to a man, as a man speaks to his fellow, does not apply a predicate contradictory to the subject.

It is true that our experience of conveying information by means of speech is confined to individuals endowed with organs of speech and hearing, such as we find possessed by man. None of us has an experience of individuals otherwise organised, that consist of an absolutely different clay, or that consist of no clay at all. Consequently, no one has observed by his organs of sensation the Deity, in whose existence, we may assume, we confidently believe. We conceive God as unendowed, or, rather, unencumbered, with those instruments of sensibility without which, our experience teaches us, man could not be what he is. Man's modes of communication with man are the only ones that come within our experience. But the fact that God exists, but is not possessed of the organs for communcation with which we are acquainted, and the operations of which we understand, does not justify us in assuming that God is powerless to convey notions to man by means, consonant with His essence, which is not understood by us, so as to awaken within us a consciousness such as is conveyed to man by spoken words. To quote Huxley's words in another essay: "If one says that consciousness cannot exist, except in relation of cause and effect with certain organic molecules, I must ask how he knows that; and if he says it can, I must put the same question." Huxley asks how he knows, but he admits the possibility.

If it be urged that the conveyance of ideas from man to man by loud spoken words is an operation fully understood by all who have an insight into physiology of sensations, whereas the operation of a conveyance of ideas by God to man by means of spoken words is above and beyond our understanding, I repeat that this does not enter into the question of possibility, but the problem is rather one for evidence ; to wit, whether an event which is possible in itself can be proved to have actually occurred.

But the point so urged requires a closer examination. If it is said that loud words spoken by man, and heard by man, and thus conveying ideas in the mind of each other, constitute an operation which is clearly understood by all who have a knowledge of the physiology of sensation, it must be asked :

Is this really the case ?   Is it true that there is anybody who has an understanding of how ideas are
awakened in the mind by means of the senses ?

Thus far no one has solved the problem. No
one has filled up the gulf gaping between the
physical process of speech and hearing and the
consciousness which it awakens in the mind.
Scientists may be able to trace the physical
operation of cause and effect ; they may be
acquainted with the physiological action of speech
and hearing to their minutest details, they may be
able to trace step by step the changes effected by
molecules upon molecules ; they may have the laws
of acoustics at their fingers' ends, and they may be
able to put their finger upon the portion of the
brain affected by hearing. But nothing of that
knowledge will explain the next step : how the
mind becomes conscious ? To use again Huxley's
words : "Consciousness is neither matter, nor force,
nor any conceivable modification of either, however
the manifestations of the phenomena of consciousness may be connected with the phenomena known
as matter and force." The science of physiology is
unable to account for consciousness. This is the case
with all consciousness awakened by our senses ; with
the feeling of colour, of beauty, whether conveyed
by the eye, or, as in the case of music, by the ear.
We understand the physiological actions of the
organs and their intermediaries, by means of which

loud words ultimately affect the brain ; but we are ignorant of the way in which these mechanical processes cause consciousness. The great physiologist, Du Bois-Raymond, numbers the origin of simple conception by the senses among the riddles which are transcendental ; which have never been, nor ever will be solved by human understanding or knowledge.

Why then should we declare it impossible for God to speak to Moses loud words capable of being heard by man, only because we cannot understand how this can be done by a Being absolutely devoid of man's means of speaking and hearing ; when we can no more know how the mechanical action of our sensiferous organs, which we profess to know, arouses consciousness of that which is present in somebody else's consciousness by means of loud spoken words ?   We might feel inclined to declare this also impossible were it not that we have evidence of its actuality.   We must needs declare a process which we believe to be real to be possible.   But the mere possibility could not be denied even without such proof, simply because it can be distinctly conceived, it implies no contradiction, and could, therefore, never be proved false by any demonstrative argument or abstract reasoning *a priori*.

But let us go a step further.   It might be objected that, in the case of consciousness being awakened by means of sensiferous organs, in conjunction with some outside natural forces, even if we are unable to span the last gap, to understand how mechanical actions affect mental properties, we do at least understand those mechanical actions themselves. We understand how causes and effects follow each other, how every effect has its certain cause; we understand the nature of the causes, the way in which they act, so as to be followed by their effects. Whereas, in the case of direct revelation we do not know of any mechanical action; we do not know whether any such action takes place; we know of the receptive faculty of hearing, but we have no knowledge of the active mode of speech. This is truly no contradiction in terms, but does it not sound very much like one? How can we speak of incidents, the supposed working of which is like a closed book to us, in the same breath with incidents of the operations of which we have examined every winch and lever, the mechanism of which is fully understood?

Fully understood! Is it, indeed? I ought to be ashamed to repeat that which ought to be considered a truism by all who have done no more than approach the boundaries of scientific research. The physiology of sensation is only one section of the vast army of phenomena, the exploration of which occupies the attention of the scientists. Science has outgrown the conception that there is nothing in the universe except matter and force; that matter and force can be, and are, understood as to their substance and functions. Force is the cause of motion, and how are we to understand its effect on matter? Does matter consist of atoms, of minute substances, so minute that they escape the observation of the sharpest eyesight, even when armed with what Mr. Samuel Weller would call a "pair o' patent double million magnifyin' gas microscopes of hextra power," and which are compact, solid, and incapable of further subdivision? In that case matter is a collection of separate existences, situated one by the side of the other. If separate, there must be space between them. In other words, they are separated by nothingness. And now we are asked to assume, nay, we are supposed to understand, that these separate existences attract and repel each other through this nothingness. Is then matter identical with force, and does the one differ from the other in name only? In that case the atoms would be something that was acting where it is not. Or has force an existence apart from matter? If so, we should be compelled to assume the existence of entities, which are indivisible, and which nevertheless occupy space, and that one atom affects the other by means of force, which has its place in nothingness.

What then are matter and force after all? They are formulæ, by the aid of which the scientists seek

to interpret the phenomena of nature ; they belong
to the hypotheses by which the scientist strives to
understand nature.   But as little as we understand
how mechanical actions arouse consciousness in the
mind, just as little do we understand how the
assumed atoms affect one another by means of the
assumed force.

Whilst reading on these subjects, quotations induced me to peruse a collection of papers which
passed between the philosopher Leibnitz and Dr.
Samuel Clarke, Rector of St. James's, in 1715 and
1716.   Dr. Clarke's object was really to take up the
cudgels for some of the propositions of Isaac
Newton's.   The question ventilated there is, whether
space is a substance or not ; space having been compared by Newton to the sensorium of God.   I shall
not trouble my readers any further with these letters
beyond quoting a few sentences.   Clarke avers
that " nothing can any more act where it is not
present than it can be where it is not."   Leibnitz
maintains that " the attraction of bodies, properly
so called, is a miraculous thing, since it cannot be
explained by the nature of bodies."   He is of opinion
that, " if God made a general law that bodies should
attract each other, it could not be put into execution
but by perpetual miracles."   Leibnitz denies the
existence of both atoms and of a vacuum.   He
holds that " the least corpuscle is actually subdivided *in infinitum*."   " What reason," he says,

"can anyone assign for confining nature in the progression of subdivision? These are fictions, merely arbitrary, and unworthy of true philosophy. The reasons assigned for a vacuum are mere sophisms." And against Leibnitz's negation of the existence of atoms, Clarke argues . . . "If there are no such perfectly solid particles (atoms), then there is no matter at all. For, the further the division and subdivison of the parts is carried, before you arrive at parts perfectly solid and without pores, the greater is the proportion of pores to solid matter in that body. If, therefore, carrying on the division *in infinitum*, you never arrive at parts solid and without pores, it will follow that all bodies consist of pores only, without any matter at all, which is a manifest absurdity."

And where will all such subtle reasoning, either on the one side or on the other, lead to? In my opinion, it will lead absolutely nowhere. But it shows how some of the keenest intellects groped in the dark in their attempts to comprehend that which is incomprehensible. We know matter and force only as forms of consciousness; they are formulæ, indispensable to the interpretation of the phenomena of nature. But who can say that he understands the nature of their substance, if substance they have? We need not go so far as Berkeley did, and assert that there is no substance of matter, but only a substance of mind. We may conceive them;

by all means let us firmly believe in their existence
as substance. But we cannot understand their
nature, much less can we say that we are able to
comprehend how they affect each other. As Du
Bois Raymond said, it is impossible for us to
understand the substance of matter and force ; they
are transcendental ; they transcend the capacity of
the human understanding. Shall we ever be able to
understand them ? The same physiologist answers
ignorabimus, We never shall.

We conceive but cannot understand either re-
pulsion or attraction. We conceive but cannot
understand force, the cause of motion. We are
conscious of causation ; we deny the existence of
uncaused effects, but we do not understand the way
in which causes produce effects. Suppose we are
attempting to speak loud human words to our
friends ; they hear them, and become conscious of
the ideas which they presume to express. But
there are two things about them which we cannot
understand.

In the first place, we do not understand how it
comes to pass that such words bring about such
consciousness in their minds, even were we able
to trace, step by step, the physical phenomena
observable in the complicated journey from those
organs within us that produce speech to the brains
of our hearers.

In the second place, the very physical movements of the organs of speech and hearing, and of everything that lies between them, transcend our understanding. Are we, therefore, to assume that such speaking and hearing cannot have any reality in fact, simply and solely because we can only conceive them, but will neither be able to understand them nor to prove their existence? If it is averred that it is impossible to understand that God speaks out loud human words, that He spoke to Moses what we read in the Pentateuch, as a man may speak to his fellow, because we do not know the nature of His substance, the answer can only be, it is true, it transcends our understanding. And if it is averred that it is impossible to understand how a man speaks to his fellow because we do not know the nature of his substance, the answer must equally be, it is true, it transcends our understanding. But if it is said that "God cannot reveal Himself in the absolute way which the orthodox conception implies," I ask, how can this impossibility be proved? It may be said, perhaps, that the proofs which I ventured to adduce for the "possibility" of such an eventuality are for the most part negative proofs. This may be so. But the "impossibility" cannot be proved either positively or negatively.

Or will this be brought forward as a proof of this impossibility, that we have never observed consciousness except in connection with matter, and by means of the senses? But, in the first place, matter itself is only known to us as a form of our consciousness ; secondly, the circumstance that we have never before experienced a certain contingency is no proof, either that others may not have had such experience, or that we, or those who come after us, may not witness it at some future time. We are here again landed in the region of evidence, or of probability, and not of possibility ; and thirdly, do we not observe innumerable phenomena in the form of consciousness which have no existence in any form of matter we may conceive ?

In conclusion, I maintain that there is no ground for saying that it is impossible for God to "reveal Himself in the absolute way which the orthodox conception implies." No such impossibility has been proved or can be proved. If we asked : granting the possibility of a direct revelation, how are we to explain such action ? I am quite willing to admit that we cannot explain it. And, in the same way, if we are asked, granting the possibility of the physical phenomena, which we observe every moment of our lives, how are we to explain the action of which these phenomena are the results ? We must again admit that we cannot explain it. No human mind can grasp the nature of God, the nature of His substance, the way in which He works. No more do we understand the nature of the substratum, the existence of which we assume, and of the activity of which we believe all physical phenomena to be the resultant. We admit the possibility of that activity in spite of our inability to comprehend it.

The possibility of a direct revelation once admitted, it then becomes a question about its reality, about its existentiality. We believe we possess irrefragable evidence of the reality of physical action, of its existentiality. In regard to a direct revelation by God, the question arises, first, what evidence have we that it has actually taken place; and, secondly, what evidence is there to show which of the several alleged revelations is the one which has actually occurred.

At this point I break off. The question of evidence has become of value once the notion of impossibility has been set aside. This latter result was the object I set myself to attain in this paper. I do not pretend to have exhausted the subject. The question of evidence cannot possibly be approached from the nature of the Deity, which we cannot comprehend, in the same way as the question of evidence of physical action cannot be explained from the nature of what we call matter, which we understand as little. To arrive at the question of evidence we must rather turn to our consciousness; to the requirements of the human soul; to the capacity of the human mind to acquire certain results without assistance from without. The enquiry would lead us to investigate whether evolution, or any similar theory, is sufficient to explain the acquisition by man of the pure notions about God and His unity.   Many topics of kindred nature would have to be investigated ; and by the conclusions thus arrived at the historical evidence in our possession would have to be tested.

But this can be mentioned only by the way, it being outside the scope of this paper.   The question of possibility once being settled, the question of evidence follows as a subject of its own.

THE MISHNAH

THE Bible forms the point round which everything that refers to Jewish life centres. The radiations that issue from it, and the rays that return to it as to a focus, have a twofold nature. They penetrate both action and thought. The precepts enjoined and frequently alluded to in the Bible by the merest hint exercised the mind of the Jew, anxious as he was to obey them, not merely to the letter but also according to their intention. The laws which made every action of life, from the cradle to the grave, an act of pontifical worship, were weighed and considered. The letter never became a dead letter. That which we call Tradition was the life-long practice by generation upon generation of that which, together with the letter, constituted the life of the Jew from time out of memory. To study, to teach, to observe, to perform, was not so much the watchword of the Jew as the Jews' second nature. The objection sometimes heard, as to how it is possible for the Jew to fathom, within the short span of life, the hundreds of precepts which, with their detailed observances, come to number thousands, is a futile objection. The Jew, brought up from infancy, by training and example, in the observance of the Law, spontaneously obeyed its behests and shunned that which it forbade.

But the meditation on God's word was to the Jew not less a divine injunction than any other precept. The study of the Bible for the sake of elucidating every detail of the divine Law was not merely the business of a class but the duty of every Jew. Theology there was, but there should not be theologians.

This at once implies that a distinction was drawn between the books of the Pentateuch and the other parts of the Bible. The five Books of Moses were considered the immediate word of God, whilst the other books contained only indirect revelation, either through prophecy or through divine inspiration. The Books of Moses were the authority for the Law : all possible injunctions were, by implication, contained in these books, in which there was nothing either missing or superfluous. The study of these laws was the study of life, to be passed at the hands of that divine guidance, and the results of that study were technically called the Halachoth in the aggregate ; the Halachah, the way of life.

Such men as made it the business of their life to scrutinize the Book and all that it contained were, in the earliest times, called "Soferim," "Scribes." Several theories have been put forward by modern scholars to explain that title, and I cannot help thinking that some of them shoot wide of the mark.

The meaning of that title seems simple enough. It is one of the most honoured titles in Israel. The "Widsom of the Scribes," of which the Mishnah, or some old Beraitha (Sotah, 15) speaks, can, according to Ben-Sira (38, 34, *seq.*) be obtained only by him who can devote all his leisure to it. The word "Soferim" is frequently used in the Talmud. The "families of Soferim," mentioned in the first book of the Chronicles (2, 55), were probably such as devoted themselves pre-eminently to the study of the Torah. The "ready Scribe," alluded to in the 45th Psalm (v. 2), does not signify merely a skilful caligraphist, or an accurate copyist. The word "Sofer," denotes one who is penetrated with the knowledge of the "Sefer," the "Book," the Book of the Torah. It was the honourable title of Ezra : he was the "ready Scribe" in the "Torah of Moses" (Ezra 7. 6.), " Ezra the priest, the Scribe, a Scribe of the words of the Commandments of God, and of His statutes to Israel " (*ibid*, 7.11, of Nehem. 8, 8.13). It was an illustrious title, the title by which Moses himself was honoured. Thus, we are told that when Moses died, a voice from on high went forth over the length and breadth of the camp of Israel, and bewailed the death of משה ספרא רבא : Moses the great Scribe." (The great Scribe: Talmud and Targumim, *passim*.)

And yet, in the course of time, the title of Sofer only then conveyed the highest praise when its bearer was at the same time recognised as the חכם, the "Sage." Only he was an authority who had risen above the mere knowledge of the words of the text and their meaning, and had mastered the intricacies of the arguments on which the Law rested. Without such attainment the Sofer ranked below the Sage. R. Eliezer Hagadol said that "since the destruction of the holy temple the Sages came only to be 'Scribes.'" The greatness of R. Meir was said to consist in this that he combined the qualities of Sage and Scribe.[1] For great as the merit was of him who had mastered the Book, who could evolve the Law from the wording of the Text after the method of the Midrash—in the oldest sense of the word—in one word, however great one may be as a "Darshan," as an expert in Midrash, in the hermeneutic of the Text, he was really great who could, at the same time, account for the "reasons" on which the deductions were based, and for the arguments for preferring one deduction above another—who was great in Talmud—this word again taken in its oldest sense—who was at the same time a דרשן, a Darshan, and a חכם, a Sage. Thus were the great teachers in Israel, Shemaiah and Abtalion, called great Sages and great Darshanim. (b. Pesachim 70b).

In the earliest traceable times the Law was propagated in the first instance as Midrash, as an

1. b. Gittin, 67a.

exegesis of Holy Writ. Whenever the Law was
read in public, an oral interpretation accompanied
it. It was the חכמים, the Sages, the σοφισταί, the
ἐξεγηταί τῶν νόμων of Josephus, or the νόμων ἑρμηνεῖς of
Philo, the Sages and the Scribes, that promulgated
the traditional laws to their hearers. The principles
inculcated by these masters were studied by a
number of disciples, who sat at their feet, who
"served" them, who ministered unto them, as it
was termed. The חכמים, the Sages, were the true
masters, who propagated their teachings to their
followers. These were the תלמידי חכמים, the students
of the Sages. Sages themselves, who ministered to
their masters, even as Joshuah, the servant of Moses,
became his successor, even as the prophet Elisha
was worthy to succeed his Master Elijah "on whose
hands he had poured water."

Great were the numbers of students who received
in this way the traditions from the "Fathers," the
קבלה or the מסרת מהאבות, the διαδοχή, συπαράδοσις τῶν
πατέρων or from the "Elders," הזקנים, παράδωσις τῶν
πρεσβυτερων. The study of "Mikra," or the text, and of
"Midrash," which aimed at its interpretation in all its
manifold theoretical and practical bearings, was
combined with "Talmud" and "Mishnah." That is
to say, the Midrashic study of the Text included the
argumentative method, "Talmud," and the concrete
enunciations of the precepts, "Mishnah." Mishnah
is the name of each law enunciated in precise terms,

of which collections were made in very early times. These collections were themselves called Mishnah, or, in the plural, Mishnioth. Only scant notices are extant of the Mishnioth of antiquity, of such collections as existed before Shammai and Hillel. There must have been a great amount; as many as six hundred or even seven hundred separate Sedarim, or arrangements, are mentioned; figures often looked upon as hyperbolical, but on no sufficient grounds. However, only one collection, the one started at the initiative of R. Jehuda Hanasi and his associates and completed by them, has come down to us in its entirety.

That collection, "our" Mishnah, offers a body of precise enunciations, ranging over the whole field of written and traditional law. It is true it contains passages which are altogether in the style of Midrash, in which the issue is taken from a distinct text. We also find occasionally arguments and discussions in which some scholars defend their views with great acumen, and which, therefore, belong to the region of Talmud. There are also passages in which the line of strict Halachah is deviated from, and which contain moral and religious reflections and therefore properly belong to the Agadah. Some Beraitoth were inserted after the work had been completed. But all such passages taken together are not numerous; moreover, with the exception of one treatise, that of Aboth, they are only thinly scattered

over the entire work. They do not in any way mar
the general character of the collection, which is that
of concrete enunciations of the distinct precepts of
the whole Law. Frequently a conflict of opinions
on one or another decision is recorded. This might
be considered to interfere with the codificatory significance of the book. So it does ; nor can the Mishnah
be called a code of law, such as, for instance, it was
the intention of Maimonides or of R. Josef Kara to
offer. The circumstance that conflicting views are
inserted in a work which aimed at presenting final
decisions, הלכה פסוקה, is explained in this way : that
it was the authors' intention to show that adverse
opinions had not been overlooked ; that any
decision, as given in the Mishnah, should not be set
aside because one or another great Sage had decided
differently, unbeknown to the authors. The latter
had, therefore, to take note of such opinions, so as
to make it clear that they had been carefully weighed
by them. But such deviations from the strict
enunciatory and codifying method can also be
explained from the compilatory nature of the work.

We know that our Mishnah is the work of R.
Jehuda, the Prince, and his associates. But it were
a mistake to assume that they were its authors in
the accepted sense of the word. They were its
compilers. Many portions are verbatim reproductions of parts of previous works, some of
which were of the same strictly Halachic nature ;

whilst others bore, more or less, a Talmudic, a Midrashic, or a Halachic character, or combined two or more of these aspects. This circumstance accounts for the fact that the Mishnah, although intending to codify and distinctly to enunciate the laws, does not outwardly bear that character in a stereotyped form, but encroaches frequently in its style upon kindred methods. We meet with such references as "the first Mishnah," "the Mishnah of R. Akiba," "the Mishnah of R. Eliezer ben Jacob," etc., but it is difficult to determine how much of the more ancient collections is contained in our Mishnah. The relation of our Mishnah to R. Jehuda Hanasi, of this Sage to R. Meir, of the latter to R. Akiba, is clear enough, yet it is difficult to allocate in detail the various elements of our Mishnah.

It is recorded that every decision of the Mishnah is, unless stated otherwise, attributable to R. Meir, who himself reproduced the teaching of his Master, R. Akiba. The latter was the fountain-head to whom not only the Mishnaic doctrines must be referred back ; he was equally the authority upon whom the Tosefta, the Sifra, and the Sifre were based.

Every phase of R. Akiba's career was of a unique character. No particulars about the years of his youth are known, for the simple reason that they were not worth knowing. It is stated that he was of pagan descent, untaught, rude, and possessed by that aversion which the uncultured feel against the scholars of the Torah. He was a shepherd, and tended the herds of a certain Kalba Sabua, a rich and benevolent man. He served his master honestly, and it was his master's daughter, Rachel, who discovered the high qualities of intellect and mind that lay dormant in her father's servant. The shepherd and the rich maiden loved each other, but she made it a condition that she would not belong to him unless he changed his mode of life and devoted himself to the study of the Torah. A secret marriage took place, and R. Akiba, who had already reached the years of mature manhood, left his bride to study under the great masters of his time. He had first to master the very elements, the Luach, the Alphabeth in its various combinations. He was not discouraged by the consciousness of his ignorance. Once he stood by a well and saw a stone that had been hollowed out. He asked who has made this stone hollow? The answer was, the rain-drops had done it. Then he thought, if so soft a substance as raindrops can hollow out a hard stone, then surely will the weighty words of the Torah penetrate my heart. During the years of his study he had to struggle with the direst poverty, for his father-in-law, having heard of the clandestine marriage, had disinherited his daughter and driven her from his house. Poor as she was herself, she strove to support her husband, even by selling her orna-mental head-dress. After twelve years of study, when returning with a large retinue of disciples, he heard an old man say jeeringly to his (R. Akiba's) wife, How much longer wilt thou pine away thy life as a husbandless wife? The answer was that, if it depended on her, she would willingly wait another twelve years if such delay tended to further accomplish her husband in the knowledge of Torah. R. Akiba acted upon that wish, returned to his studies, and came home at last with a great following as a famous Master in Israel. His wife went to meet him and wished to prostrate herself at his feet, but, poorly clad as she was, the servants wanted to restrain her, but R. Akiba said : Let this noble woman come near, for whatever I am, whatever you are this day, it is all due to her instigation and self-sacrifice. Meanwhile, Kalba Sabua, having regretted his rash vow, on hearing that a great Sage had arrived, wished to consult him as to its validity. He placed the matter before R. Akiba, who asked him whether he would have made his vow had he foreseen that his son-in-law would at some future time distinguish himself as a Master in the Torah? The answer was that he would have willingly consented to his daughter's marriage if his son-in-law had a knowledge of one treatise, or even one Halachah. Know then, replied R. Akiba, that I am that son-in-law whom thou hast rejected on account of his ignorance. Needless to say that a complete reconciliation followed.

Returning to R. Akiba's career. In the first place, he was a master of research. He had acquired the whole material of the Tradition by collecting, searching out, and storing in his mind all that had been delivered by those before him. Secondly, he was the expounder of the Law to large numbers of disciples. Thirdly, he was the great systematiser. His knowledge was not a store of promiscuous learning. Whenever he acquired some fresh information, his first care was to recognise its character, to take note of the method by which it was deduced, and to assign it to the class of subjects to which it properly belonged. He imparted his knowledge in the same methodical manner, hence his fitness to be a teacher. He kept the boundary lines of the various traditional modes of cognition : Midrash, Halachah, Agadah, severely apart. R. Jehuda Hanasi compared him to a workman going to market with a box, into which he put such products as he might purchase, wheat, barley, spelt, lentils, but who, on coming home, carefully sifts the contents of his box, and puts the wheat apart, the barley apart, the beans apart, the lentils apart. This was R. Akiba's method. He arranged all the departments of the Torah, each according to its appropriate character. He used to transmit the Torah to his pupils in this systematic way. (*Toseftah Zabim*, I, 5.)

R. Jehuda Hanasi bore, as the principal compiler

of the Mishnah, the same relation to R. Meir as the latter bore to R. Akiba. However careful the Sages always were never to fail to mention the source of their information, yet it is recorded that R. Meir did not deem it necessary to give R. Akiba's name, although he scrupulously mentioned R. Ishmael's name when his knowledge was derived from that Master. In the case of R. Akiba it was unnecessary, because it was universally known that R. Meir had acquired the bulk of his knowledge from him. (J. Berachot, 2.) The same is the case with R. Jehuda Hanasi in reference to R. Meir. Where no authority is named in our Mishnah, we know that, with few exceptions, we have directly R. Meir's views and indirectly those of R. Akiba.

We have said that the Mishnah contained principally the Law, or rather, the Laws, in their concrete enunciation. It might be expected, therefore, that the Mishnah repeated in a codified form all the precepts contained in the Pentateuch. But this is by no means the case. We do not find such enunciations as, for instance, The seventh day shall be kept holy, work is prohibited on that day, the eating of unclean animals is prohibited, clean animals are such as both chew the cud and are cloven-footed, it is prohibited to steal, it is prohibited to murder, etc., etc. Nothing of the kind will be found. The Mishnah does not contain the elementary notions of precepts and prohibitions.

Take as an example the treatise of Sabbath. The Mishnaic enunciations start from a basis which posits, as already known, not only the general injunctions regarding the Sabbathical laws, but also the various precepts that emanate from them. The Mishnah presupposes as known the results arrived at by Tradition, and confines itself to the classification, the limitations, and the definitions of these results. The Mishnah is not a textbook for the religious instruction of the young, but it is a book to guide laymen and judges in the execution of all the observances which comprise Jewish life, in its religious, social, economical, and domestic relations. The Mishnah does not deem it necessary to tell us that we must keep the Sabbath, nor even that keeping the Sabbath means omitting this and doing that. All this is presumed to be known. The Mishnah of Sabbath starts at once with definitions, qualifications, and limitations. There certainly is an enumeration of thirty-nine actions which constitute work in a Sabbathical sense, but these are only categories or " Fathers," as the Mishnaic idiom terms them, under which all varieties of work have to be classified. Besides, the enumeration itself is only incidental. Namely, the Law draws a distinct line of demarcation between that which is, indeed, prohibited but the commission of which has no further practica consequences, and that which entails interference by the authorities or some expiatory action on the part of the sinner. A person may be an offender in the former direction without being accountable in the latter sense. He may even be liable, but not for each action, several of which may entail only one liability. It is only incidental on the consideration of these aspects that the thirty-nine categories are enumerated so as to describe them and to fix their limitations. The Mishnah does not say " do not build on the Sabbath," " do not prepare food on the Sabbath," but it defines that which constitutes building or preparing food, and tells us when such actions have, or have not, penal or expiatory consequences. That which is explained here—rather fully, for the sake of giving an example—in regard to the Sabbatical injunctions, applies equally to the whole body of the laws. We thus never find that Mishnah and Pentateuch overlap each other, while Mishnah and Talmud or Mishnah or Midrash, do so only in the minority of cases.

Our Mishnah, the Mishnah of R. Jehuda Hanasi, presents, in its present shape, a compact body, and is as homogeneous as a compilation ever can be. The Language of the Mishnah is new Hebrew ; as a matter of fact, it is a distinct dialect of Hebrew. Taking the Hebrew of the Bible as the standard specimen of pure Hebrew, or, rather, of Hebrew in its living form, the language of the Mishnah presents such a modification as follows naturally, when elements, such as familiarity with a kindred dialect, homeliness of expression, evanescence of certain grammatical distinctness, combine to form a fresh dialect of the old tongue. The influence of Aramaic is considerable ; it supplies the Mishnah with a great portion of its vocabulary. Many words that are of purely Hebrew origin assume Aramaic terminations or inflections. Yet the language of the Mishnah is by no means an Aramaic but decidedly a Hebrew dialect. Besides such Biblical words as occur bearing the same meaning as in the Bible, it contains also a rich vocabulary which, though not Biblical, is yet unalloyed Hebrew. The Latin and Greek words occurring in the Mishnah refer for the most part to government, law, medicine, coins, trade, and articles of food.

The diction of the Mishnah is clear, brief, precise ; more so even than is usually met with in modern codes of legislation. Its terseness reminds one rather of the style employed in military commands. There is no circumlocution, there are no involved sentences, and "the smallness of the number of particles, and the prevalence of the simple co-ordination of clauses without periodic structure," which is a common characteristic of most Semitic languages, has reached in the Mishnah the utmost verge of possibility.

The Mishnah consists of six parts, called "Sedarim," "Arrangements." From the initials of

"Shisha," meaning six, and "Sedarim," meaning
arrangements, the work obtained the designation of
"Shas." Each of these parts is divided into Treatises
(מסכתות), each of which is subdivided into chapters
(פרקים). The first arrangement is called "Zeraim"
(זרעים), "Seeds." It contains the laws incidental
upon agriculture. At the head of this portion, and
therefore at the head of the whole Shas, is placed
the treatise of "Berachoth" (ברכוח) "Blessings." It
worthily heralds the great structure of divine legislation. The worship of God that pervades the
whole of Jewish existence must issue from the
heart; which to direct again to God is the ultimate
object of the whole legislation. It is said : How
does the service of the heart manifest itself ? By
prayer." The treatise that heads the collection
deals, therefore, with the regulations connected with
the "service of God with the heart." It first treats
of the duty of the reading of the Sh'ma. (Deut.
6, 4-9 : -11, 13-21 : Numbers 15, 37-41.) As it
was pointed out before, the Mishnah neither enters
upon an explanation of these Pentateuchal sections,
nor does it give an exposition of the religious
bearings of the regular, daily recital. All that is
assumed to be known. It plunges at once *in medias
res*, it starts with concrete enunciations of regulations
about the time within which such recital can be said
to be a fulfilment of the duty of "Reading the
Sh'ma," and the benedictions that are to precede

and follow the "Reading," the formulæ of the benedictions again not being given, but supposed to be known. This is followed by an enumeration of duties of such urgency that on their account the reading may be interrupted, or even suspended. Of these, the duties attendant upon burying the dead are the foremost. Regulations about prayers follow, a few of which are worthy of particular mention. We must not rise to pray except in a spirit of deep humility. The pious men of old used to pause an hour before praying, so as to direct their hearts to God. Even should the king greet him he should not answer, even should a snake coil round his ankle he should not be interrupted. The manifestation of God's power in rain must be mentioned in the benediction for the revival of the dead; a prayer for dew and rain is inserted in the prayer for a fertile year. The subsequent chapters deal with benedictions before and after food, and with those to be pronounced on various occasions. For beneficent rains, and on hearing good tidings, the formula is, "Blessed be He who is good and beneficent," and on hearing evil tidings, it runs, "Blessed be the true judge." He who prays regarding things which have already happened utters a vain prayer. We are bound to bless God for evil, in the same way as for benefit received, for it is said : Thou shalt love the Lord, thy God, with all thy heart, with all thy soul, and with all thy might.

"With all thy heart" means with both thy
inclinations, with the good and evil inclinations;
with all thy soul—even if He take thy life; with
all thy might—with all thy property. . . . No
one may behave irreverently before the Eastern
gate of the temple, which is in a line with the Holy
of Holies! No one must walk on the temple
mountain with his stick, his girdle of money, or
with dust on his feet, he must not make it a
thoroughfare; much less may he spit there. . . . It
was ordained that one should greet his friend with
the name of God, as it is said: (Ruth 2.4) "And
Boaz came from Bethlehem, and said unto the
reapers, the Lord be with you, and they answered
him, the Lord bless thee"; and further it is said
(Judges 6.12) "The Lord be with you, thou mighty
man of valour." Moreover, it is said (Prov. 23.22)
"Despise not thy mother when she is old"; and
(Ps. 119.126) "It is time for the Lord to work: they
have made void thy Law." R. Nathan explains this
verse thus: "They have made void thy Law because
it is time to work for the Lord." Thus the treatise
ends.

These brief excerpts from the first treatise must
suffice; it is impossible to do more now than to give
the general drift of the six Sedarim, except for
making a few remarks in reference to one or two
treatises. The Seder Zeraim, "Seeds," gives after
the above named treatise the religious laws con-

nected with agricultural pursuits. The second arrangement, "Moed," "Seasons," gives the duties connected with the solemn days all the year round. The third, "Nashim," "Women," contains the laws regarding matrimonial life in all its bearings. The fourth, "Nezikin," "Damages," comprises the whole of Jewish jurisprudence. The fifth, "Kadoshim," "Holy things," contains the sacerdotal laws, and the sixth, "Taharots," "Purifications," presents the laws of purity and impurity in the religious sense of the terms.

A few words ought to be said in regard to three treatises because of the peculiar interest attached to them. The Mishnah is, above all, a book of laws. Whereas the laws of other nations refer exclusively to the relations of the individuals towards each other, and to the social and political structure at large, the divine laws of the Pentateuch pervade every phase and aspect of Jewish life. Whilst other nations consider it imperative to bring the greatest acumen to bear on questions as between man and his neighbour, the Jew considers it his duty to investigate with equal earnestness the details of the divine precepts. It is, therefore, surprising that the forbidding aspects by which law books usually repel a casual reader are so frequently mitigated in the books of the Mishnah. A forensic purist might even urge that it was a great fault in a work, which ought to be neither more nor less than a law book,

K

to insert moral reflections, historical allusions, and sparks of religious fervour. But so it is. The architectural dimensions of that temple of Jewish legislature are frequently outlined by a pleasing display of floral decorations. But the Mishnah does not stop there. One of the courts of the temple consists of a beautifully laid out garden, where the mind of the Jew is refreshed, inspired, consoled, and elevated. It is the collection known as the treatise of "Aboth," "The Chapters of the Fathers." This treatise may, or, perhaps, must have originally presented a somewhat different form from that which it has now in our collection; but on the whole its arrangement was essentially the same as it is now. It is unnecessary to dwell on the con-jectures of those who endeavour to assign certain parts of the Treatise to certain distinct sages. Suffice it to say that the assumption which recom-mended itself to many scholars, that the sole purpose for which the first two chapters were written was to give a chronology of the first Sages, and to show thereby the continuity of the Tradition, cannot, it appears, stand the test of further reflection. The sayings of these Sages were not recorded for the purpose of registering their names ; it was the weight and impressiveness of the sayings that was the motive for recording them.

The treatise opens with the statement that the Torah, received by Moses on Sinai, was transmitted by him to Joshuah, from him to the Elders, then to the prophets and the men of the great assembly, of whom Simon the Just was one of the last survivors. " He (Simon the Just) used to say that the world is stayed on three supports : on the Torah, on the Worship, and on acts of benevolence." Of his successor, Antigonus of Socho, the following dictum is mentioned : " Be not like servants, who minister to the Lord with a view of receiving recompense, but like servants who minister to the Lord without a view of receiving recompense, and let the fear of Heaven be upon you." Sayings of the five pairs follow. Namely, in previous generations, up to Shammai and Hillel, there had been only one disputed law, referring to a detail of sacerdotal practices, and this disagreement was continued in the discussions of five successive pairs of Sages, one of whom was the Nasi, and the other the Ab-Beth-Din (President of the court). A maxim of each of these ten Sages is preserved. They are couched in an aphoristic form, brief, concise, full of wisdom, of self-denial, of love of God, of love of the Torah, love of one's fellow men. " Let thy house be a meeting place for the wise." . . . " Let thy house be opened wide, and let the poor be thy household." . . . " Judge every man in the scale of merit." . . . " Keep free from an evil neighbour, and associate not with the wicked." . . . " While the litigants stand before thee, let them be in thine eyes as guilty, and when dismissed from thee, let them be in thine eyes as righteous." . . . "Make a full examination of the witnesses, and be guarded in thy words, lest from them they might learn to lie." (These two last aphorisms refer to Judges). . . . "Ye wise men, be guarded in your words, lest you incur the penalty of exile." . . . "Be of the disciples of Aaron, loving peace, and bringing men nigh unto the Torah." . . . "Say little and do much, and receive every man with a pleasant expression of countenance."

After the "five Pairs" four generations are mentioned, which group themselves round the name of R. Jehuda Hanasi, the chief compiler of our Mishnah, namely, his grandfather, his father, himself, and his son. R. Jehuda Hanasi said, "Which is the right course which one should choose for himself ? That which tends to honour him who pursues it, and for which others honour him. Be as scrupulous about a light precept as about a grave, and reckon the loss incurred by the fulfilment of a duty against its reward, and the gain from a sin against its loss. And consider three things, and thou wilt be preserved from sin. Know what is above thee: an eye that sees, an ear that hears, and all thy deeds being written in a book." After some maxims of R. Gamliel, R. Jehuda Hanasi's son, the sayings of the older Tannaim are resumed, commencing with Hillel's warnings : "Separate not thyself from the congregation, and trust not thyself until the day of thy death, and judge not thy fellow until thou comest into his place." Apophtegms of R. Jochunan ben Zakkai and his most eminent disciples are followed by those of more than forty Sages. The fifth and last chapter contains for the most part anonymous sayings suggested by certain figures, such as ten, seven, four. By ten sayings the world was created. What can we learn from this ? Could it not have been created by one saying ? But the reason is, so that punishment may be meted out to the wicked who destroy the world that was created by ten sayings, and that a goodly reward may come to the righteous who maintain the world that was created by ten sayings. An example of Seven. Seven qualities are possessed by the uncultured, and seven by wise men. The wise man does not speak before him who is greater in wisdom ; does not interrupt the words of his companion ; is not hasty in reply ; questions according to the subject matter, and answers according to the norm ; speaks on the first thing first, and on the last thing last ; says I have not heard, of that which he has not heard ; and acknowledges the truth. The opposites belong to the uncultured." An example of Four. "There are four characters of man. Who says, Mine is mine, and thine is thine, is an indifferent character ;

but some say it is the character of Sodom; who says, Mine is thine and thine is mine, is ignorant; who says, Mine and thine are thine, is pious; Mine and thine are mine, is wicked."

A few words on two more treatises. "Tamid" or "Olath Tamid," "The Daily Offering," bears a two-fold character. It is at the same time legislatory and descriptive. It graphically and historically sets forth the rites regarding the daily offerings. The priests on duty slept in the temple; the young men on the ground, the elders on ledges, holding the keys of the court in their hands. The first duty in the morning was the clearing of the altar of its ashes. The various duties were assigned to the individual priests by lot, the casting of which was superintended by the chief (Memunna). An inspection was made to ascertain that all utensils were in their proper places; the laver was raised up from the well into which it was let down every evening; and the required ablutions were made. A detailed description follows as to how the wood for the altar was brought in, how the fire was laid, and the lamb produced. Ninety-three gold and silver vessels were used, the slaughtering place was fitted with low stands called "dwarfs," which had blocks of cedar wood, provided on the top with iron hooks. As soon as the great gate was open, the cleaning of the golden altar and the candlestick was proceeded with. The lamb was offered, the prayers read, and, after some preparation, the incense was burned. "Whenever the high priest entered the Hechal—the part which lay between the court and the holy of holies —to prostrate himself, three (priests) held him, one on his right hand, one on his left, and one over the precious stones (which were on the shoulder pieces of the Ephod). When the Memunna heard the sound of his footsteps, he lifted the curtain for him. Then the high priest entered the Hechal, prostrated himself, and went out, after which his brother priests did the same. After the prayers had been read, and the afore-mentioned services performed, the priests blessed the people (Numbers 6. 24-26). The treatise concludes with a description of the last acts of the offerings for the day, and an account of the psalms that were sung on the different days of the week. "On the Sabbath they recited Ps. 92. A psalm, a song for the Sabbath day. A psalm, a song for the world to come, for the day of complete rest and tranquillity in the eternal life."

Still more remarkable is the treatise of " Middoth," "Measurements." The treatise is very old. Whilst R. Meir is tacitly adopted as the authority in the greatest part of the Mishnah, R. Eliezer ben Jacob, who lived before him, is named as the bearer of this treatise. Like Tamid, the Mishnah of Middoth starts with a description of the watch kept in the temple during the night. The priests watched in three, and the Levites in twenty-one places. The superintendent patrolled the various points, and woe to the sentinel who was found asleep at his post. The situation and measurements of the gates are given in detail, as also those of the place of fire, the temple mount, the inner and outer courts and walls, the altar, the slaughtering place, the laver, the temple proper, with all its various chambers, offices, appointments, and gangways; particularly the "Lishkath Hagazith," the chamber of hewn stones. The description and measurements of the temple, as given in the treatise of Middoth, are minute, and what is more, they are correct. They have stood the test of ages; they have been verified by modern research and excavations on the spot. It is true that Josephus also produced a description of the temple, but—says Sir Charles Warren (*Underground Jerusalem*, London, 1876, pp. 73-79): "The temple is not well described by Josephus; the account in the Mishnah is far more explicit and appears to be very correct. The Talmudic account can be taken in preference, for, whenever there is a disagreement with Josephus, the internal evidence shows the latter to be in error. The Mishnah measurements appear to have been taken on the spot. . . . The gates, according to the Talmud, were 46¾ cubits from centre to centre, and this entirely agrees with the position of the tunnels on the ground."

We have here only touched the fringe of the

subject. The general reader has many opportunities of making himself acquainted with the Agadic portions of Talmudic literature, whilst the Halachic portions are either accessible to students only, or repel the outsider by the strictly objective nature of their contents. This is one of the causes why so strange ideas obtain about the Talmud. It is not understood that the Halachah, when considered in its historical aspect, represents the life of the Jew in all its relations. If ever a literature mirrors the life of a race in all its religious, social, and individual bearings, it is the Talmudic literature. The precepts of the Pentateuchal legislation, in their traditional extension, are the signs by which the Jew steers his way through life, and the oldest, and at the same time the most concise exponent in their entirety which we possess is the Mishnah.

RASHI AS AN EXEGETE

A Lecture read before the Jews' College Literary Society,
February, 1906

THE Rabbinical precepts about mourning enjoin that the loss of men who during their lifetime had propagated the knowledge of the Torah in Israel be bewailed in the same way as the loss of the nearest and dearest blood relation. The mourning for such a man is not to be confined to his kindred only, but it is the duty of the whole congregation of Israel. We know how the sacred rite of commemorating the loss of a parent is performed at every anniversary of the death by the children as long as they live. But one generation goeth and one generation cometh, but Israel abideth for ever. And thus it is that, whilst the memory of the most beloved of parents must ultimately be consigned to oblivion, in spite of the warmest filial piety, the congregation of Israel is able to commemorate its great departed even after the lapse of century upon century.

Noble is the duty the fulfilment of which coincides with the spontaneous promptings of the heart. The duty of commemorating the death of a parent is to the child an impulse of the heart rather than a matter of obedience to prescribed law. It is the same when

Israel mourns the loss of one or the other of its great sons. Witness at the present day the spontaneous outburst of filial piety among Jewry all over the globe at the remembrance of the death of Rashi, which took place eight hundred years ago. Jewish scholars of note have striven, on this occasion, to rescue from oblivion relics of the mind of the great master which were lying buried among the forgotten parchments of the great libraries. Meetings have been organised in numbers of Jewish centres, in order to make known far and wide the debt which Israel owes to Rashi. Here we notice a remarkable, and, indeed, a unique phenomenon. It was not necessary to revive or to resuscitate the memory of that man, who died eight hundred years ago. Rashi's memory does not stand in need of reviving. Ever since Rashi's death, one generation went and one generation came, and Rashi has been abiding with us. It is perplexing to see how Rashi has entered into the very life of the Jew, and the question almost forces itself upon us: What then was the Jew before Rashi lived ? That question can, of course, be easily answered, but we must pass it by. Enough for us that the Bible was henceforth studied with Rashi as a guide; that no Jewish commentator who has since arisen could afford to ignore him ; that mediæval Christian commentators based their knowledge upon his teachings. And as for Mishnah and Talmud, for us, as for the generations which immediately precede us, they would have been almost sealed books. There is not the slightest exaggeration in saying this; and Rashi has achieved this by being the great exegete.

To speak about Rashi as an exegete is in reality too vast a subject for a lecture. For, as the saying was applied to the Torah, that "its measure is of greater length than the earth, vaster than the ocean," the same may be said when we wish to enter into detailed accounts about the Torah's great expounder. It would perhaps be more prudent to select a certain portion of Rashi's exegetical productions, and to speak, for instance, only on his commentary on the Pentateuch, or on some Talmudical treatise. In dealing with the whole subject, it will only be possible for me to sketch out the principal characteristics of his exegesis, so as to understand how it was that it became indispensable, and has not been made superfluous by the efforts of his successors.

For it is through his commentaries that Rashi has survived, that he has become the source from which both scholar and layman drew. Here we meet with some features which appear at first sight contradictory, and even altogether irreconcilable. First, no commentator ever strove so hard to be lucid and intelligible in his attempts to make lucid and intelligible the subject of his expositions; and yet no commentator has ever had so many super-commentators, whose object it was to clear up all that appeared obscure and difficult of understanding in the words of the master. Secondly, Rashi, in his commentaries on the Bible, and more especially in those on the Pentateuch, insists that his sole object is to set forth the Pshat, *i.e.*, the sober meanings of the words, the connection of the sentences, and hence, the natural meaning of the text according to the letter; and yet, it has been said—and apparently justly so—that he was no more than a traditional and Midrashic expositor of the Bible. Thirdly, there is the glaring difference of method between his biblical commentaries on the one hand, and those on the Talmud on the other hand. And for all that, there is an oneness in the man and his methods which, if correctly understood, accounts for all seeming incongruities.

If I were to say that all these difficulties disappear when we bear in mind that Rashi was a Jew, you might think that I was trifling with my audience. Of course Rashi was a Jew ; but there have been millions upon millions of Jews, without any of them having been a Rashi. I am afraid that I do not amend my proposition when I say that Rashi was a Jewish commentator, for so was Saadiak, Rashbam, Ramban, and a host of others of greater or lesser significance, in whose works, however, such apparently contradictory aspects cannot be observed. I must, therefore, be somewhat more explicit to make myself understood. What I mean to convey is, that Rashi, endowed with gifts which made him an ideal interpreter, represented, at the same time, in his person, all that which stamps the Jewish race with the seal of its individuality. The Jewish race has its Bible; the Bible is its book; certainly, outwardly; but to the Jew the Bible is life itself. In theory as in practice, it was his great object to read the Bible, to study the Bible; it was his greater object to live the Bible. It is his flesh and blood; it is to him what the atmosphere is to terrestrial beings; what water is to the fishes. When once the tyrannical powers made a decree by which the Jews were forbidden to occupy themselves with the study of the Torah, R. Akiba disregarded it, and he justified his disobedience by the following fable. "A fox walked once on the brink of the river, and saw the fishes darting backwards and forwards in great perturbation. The fox asked the fishes: 'Why do you flee?' They answered: 'We flee because men are casting out nets in order to catch us.' The fox thereupon said: 'Come on dry land, and you and I will live amicably together as our ancestors used to do.' And the fishes said: 'And they call thee the most cunning animal? Indeed, thou art a fool. If we have so much reason for going in fear, when we are in the element which supports our life, how much worse would it be for us were we to go outside our element, where death is certain.'" Thus R. Akiba pronounced that the life of the Jew with the Torah may be precarious, but that without it there would be no existence for him.

Certainly the Bible is a book. Like every written document it requires elucidation ; form and contents have to be scrutinised ; its language, grammar, diction have to be investigated in order to arrive at a clear understanding. This would be sufficient, to the exclusion of all indirect modes of interpetation, if the Bible were a literary product and no more. But it becomes quite different when it is considered as a guide to our conduct, permeating all phases of Jewish life. Then it is no longer a product of literature of interest to the student only, but it is of interest to everybody. The anxiety to shape life scrupulously upon the pattern of its contents makes it imperative to try to understand its meaning for the purpose of practical application. But more than this. The usages of century, upon century gave sanction to certain norms which regulate life according to the book. They are called the oral law, the traditional law, the Halacha, the way of life. They form a traditional commentary on the book ; they are a living exegesis which shows how the book has been understood from times immemorial. During the wanderings of the Jews the living commentary accompanied the dead parchment and ink, and the dead letters and words had to account for the living usages.

But to the Jew the book is even more than all this. For the Halacha, the traditional way of life, fashions the life of the Jew after the book only in his duties towards God and man. But the book, being the Jew's very nature, is as little mere food for the linguist, the historian, the anthropologist, the philosopher, as nature itself is only food for the geologist, the astronomer, the physicist, the chemist. Sunshine and sunset, fauna and flora, hills and dales, rivers and seas, in the grandeur of their aspects, in the beauty and symmetry of their details, affect the bulk of mankind in a different manner from that of the dry-as-dust investigator or patient scientist. The despondency of mind caused by a gloomy sky in a closed and confined atmosphere, the exhilaration and cheerfulness effected by a sunny day in a picturesque landscape, are outside the scope of the scientist, who would consider nature from a point of view similar to that from which the Bible is investigated merely as an item in the world of letters. But to the Jew the book had to be a substitute for the ordinary contemplation of nature. For a succession of centuries the Jews had neither sky nor landscape; they were confined within the gloomy walls of a Ghetto, within the confines of pales of settlement; there was no security of life; they were driven from pillar to post, from sky to sky, from soil to soil, when, as already the Sibyllist has said: "every land, every sea, would be full of them and their own land empty of them." The Jew was precluded from feeding his poetical and imaginative impulses with that nourishment which humanity at large derives from sky and land and water. But, לא אלמן ישראל, Israel is not forsaken; God has provided us with a substitute, מטמון באמתחותינו, a hidden treasure in our luggage, that accompanied us in all our wanderings, our Book of Books, our Torah. From the pages of that book flowers blossomed forth, bright sunshine cheered our paths; from between its lines we heard the tuneful carols of the birds, the warning sounds of thunder, the soothing murmurs of brook and rill.

This is our Midrash, the Agadic exposition of our Torah, the manna from heaven on which the poetical and imaginative instincts of the Jew fed; and all brought in connection with, all evolved from, that book which constitutes the soul of the Jew, the Torah.

In the case of nature the pure scientist investigates its phenomena, apart from all emotional, poetical, ethical, or religious bearings; his equivalent in regard to the Bible is the philological, historical, archæological expounder, who keeps exclusively and strictly to the Pshat. The mechanical scientist tries to discover how the secrets of nature can be made subservient to man, how they can be made the guides to his practical life; this, as regards the Bible, corresponds with the

Talmud in its Halachic portions. In nature, the poet and the artist attempt to give expression to the influence which it exercises upon the emotions, the poetical impulses, and the sentimental instincts ; this is the Talmud in its Agadic portions. The combination of these three elements, in greater or lesser completeness, in more or less homogeneity, formed for ages the life of the Jew. The harmonisation of these elements into such homogeneity as is within the reach of one individual was effected by Rashi in his exegesis of the Bible. This is what I meant to convey when I said that Rashi's significance lies in the fact that he was a Jew.

His natural qualifications were those without which he would never have attained an influence which outlasted ages. There was, in the first place, the impulse to impart the fruits of his own acquisitions to his brethren. Secondly, there was his self-denial, which amounted almost to self-effacement; in the mass of his exegetical remarks, the cases in which he mentions himself can, so to say, be counted on one's fingers. Thirdly, his was the gift which the ideal teacher possesses; an inexhaustible patience ; he hardly ever refers readers to other passages in his commentaries ; there are scarcely any cross references ; open a book which is accompanied by his commentary on any page, and you will almost always find the desired information, although several times given elsewhere in parallel passages. Fourthly, there is that conciseness of expression which never uses two words where one suffices; an economy and sobriety which gave rise to the saying that Rashi wrote with a pen of gold, a saying only significant before the invention of fountain pens with golden nibs, implying, as it did, that he wrote as if afraid of wearing out his pen. Another proverb to the same effect was, that at Rashi's time a drop of ink must have cost a golden piece.

The task which Rashi had set himself, in his exegesis of Scripture, of doing justice to all three elements, was prodigious beyond description. It cannot be denied that the Halachic and Agadic interpretation comes frequently into serious conflict with the sober linguistic explanation of the Pshat. It was not Rashi's plan to place the results of these various hermeneutical methods one by the side of the other, but to blend them into one harmonious whole. In the former case it would have meant the juxtaposition of different commentaries, each taken from one of these different points of view; some such method as, for instance, was applied by Ibn Ezra to his commentary, or rather, commentaries, on the Song of Solomon. But such was not Rashi's object. His aim was to expound the Bible, and particularly the five books of Moses, according to the Pshat, and to the Pshat only. He was fully alive to the necessity of explaining the text according to its merits. He was sensible of the imperative demands of grammar, of the sequence of sentences, of the correct meaning of every word. In his commentary to the Pentateuch he repeatedly uses the phrase, " My sole object is to elucidate the text according to the Pshat ; there are many Agadic explanations of the passage, but this is the Pshat." How then can this be reconciled with the many Midrashic explanations with which his Biblical commentaries abound ? Can it be that Rashi understood the term Pshat in a different sense from that which we attach to it ? This is indeed the case ; the meaning which he applied to the term offers the solution of the apparent incongruity, of aiming at the Pshat and supplying, at the same time, Midrashic and Halachic expositions.

Rashi never doubted the supreme importance of the Halachic injunctions and their close connection with the text, he never questioned the right of deriving from the letter of the text any number of religious and ethical lessons, moralising contemplations, philosophical and theosophical speculations, and to arrive at them by involved, forced, and even violent interpretation of the text. In the first place, the assumption that every word, every letter of the Torah had emanated from God Himself, led to the inference that it was lawful, that it was even demanded, to find in every phrase, in the choice of every word, in the syntactical connection of expressions, a hint that something more was implied than that which lies on the surface. Secondly, that which I called before the living commentary of the Torah, the traditional exegesis which had swayed the life of the Jew for ages, and which was not less his Torah than the written document, was to Rashi not only irrefragable truth, but was considered by him in the light of a true exposition of the word divine. And it is here that Rashi draws his distinctions; he separates such Agadic and Halachic explanations as are Pshat from such as are not Pshat. He calls Pshat such Agadic and Halachic explanations as adapt themselves to the wording of the text without doing violence to grammar, to the meaning of the terms used, and to the context. I do not mean to say that Rashi does not also call Pshat the plain meaning of the sentences which follow naturally, without regard to indirect Midrashic notions. He certainly insists on that method and calls it Pshat. But he includes in the term such Midrashim as adapt themselves to the text. He only excludes, as not deserving the name of Pshat, such Midrashim as do, in his opinion, violence to the meaning of the words and the sequence of the sentences. He admits the legitimacy of the most forced explanations, but is of opinion that, admissible as they are, they are not Pshat.

This theory will have to be proved, and it cannot be done better than by Rashi's own words. He himself sketches out that mode of proceeding, as usual, in his terse style and economical phraseology, in several passages. Thus, he says in his commentary on Genesis iii. 8: "There are many Agadic Midrashim on this verse, but they have already been arranged methodically by our Sages in Bereshith Rabba and in other Midrashic collections; my task is only to explain the Pshat of the text, and to give such Agada as elucidates the words of the text, in accordance with the natural sequence of the sentences."

The principal passage in which he explains his method is his short introduction to his commentary on the Song of Solomon. He starts with the words of the Pslamist (62, 12): "Once God has spoken, twice I have heard this," or as it is taken here: " God has spoken one thing, and I have heard two things." "One verse," he says, " branches out into several meanings, but, when everything has been considered, there is no verse which loses its plain and simple meaning. It is true, the prophets spoke their words to serve as parables, but the parable must be adapted to the wording according to its context, and to the sequence of the verses as they appear in their arrangement, one after the other. In regard to the present book (the Song of Solomon) I have seen several Midrashim to it, some of which comprise the whole book in one continuous Midrash, whilst others split it up into several Midrashim, according to the separate verses, which latter Midrashim adapt themselves neither to the wording nor to the sequence of the sentences. Therefore I resolved to grasp the literal meaning of the verses, to expound it according to the sequence of the sentences; and as for the Midrashic explanations of our Sages, I shall subjoin each Midrash to the passage to which it naturally belongs."

Thus we see that to Rashi the Pshat is the true interpretation, and so is the Midrashic explanation. Both are allowed authority, one by the side of the other. Modern scholars sometimes sneer at this method of ascribing equal admissibility to such different modes of interpretation. Others good-humouredly smile at it as a *naiveté* which they consider childish, and yet so amiable. But there is nothing to deride and nothing to condone. With the same right might the geologist and the chemist smile at the physician prescribing for his patients a change of scenery and surroundings to a more salubrious soil. To Rashi, as to many other commentators, in fact, to every Jew throughout centuries, to every preacher who inculcates moral and religious lessons with the Bible in his hand, such manifold consideration of the Bible is not only legitimate but also indispensable. But Rashi shows himself the sober-minded Darshan and expositor of the letter. He accepts in his commentaries as Pshat the Midrashic explanations which adapt themselves to the letter. He does not deny the legitimacy of such Midrashim

as are more far-fetched, and do more or less violence
to the text.   On the contrary ; but he considers them
as lying outside the boundaries which he had set
himself in his exegesis.

Once Rashi had made his standpoint clear to
himself he consistently adhered to it. He neither
looked to the right nor to the left. However great
the authority may be of a Midrash which was not
adaptable to the letter, it had no place in his commentary. Even the Talmudic Sages, for whom
he entertained unbounded veneration, were not
considered of sufficient authority for him to insert
some remote interpretation of theirs.   More than
that ; no one was more than Rashi penetrated
with the sense of obedience due to the Halachic
decisions of the Rabbis; he would never have
thought it possible to dispute the validity of
the results arrived at by certain rules, whenever
conflicting opinions occur in the Talmud on some
point of law. But even so, the indisputable Talmudic decision was to Rashi one thing and the
method which he had planned for himself was
another. And so it happens occasionally that he
explains a text which refers to Halacha in a sense
which differs from the final Talmudical decision,
merely because the interpretation which the Talmud
rejects adapts itself better to the text, without his
intending by this to impugn the validity of the
decision.

I must indulge here in a rather lengthy quotation, first, for the purpose of hearing from Rashi himself what his attitude was towards the authorities ; and, secondly, to give a specimen of what I should like to call Rashi's Agadic Pshat. You all remember the passage in Exodus, vi. 2-8 : "And God spake unto Moses and said unto him, I am the Lord. And I appeared unto Abraham, unto Isaac, and unto Jacob, as God Almighty, but by my name JHVH, I was not known to them. And I also have established my covenant with them to give them the land of Canaan, the land of their sojournings in which they sojourned. And moreover, I have heard the groanings of the children of Israel whom the Egyptians keep in bondage, and I have remembered my covenant. Wherefore say unto the children of Israel I am the Lord, and I will bring them out from under the burdens of the Egyptians, and I will rid you out of their bondage, and I will redeem you with a stretched out arm and with great judgments, and I will take you to me for a people, and I will be to you a God ; and ye shall know that I am the Lord your God, which bringeth you out from under the burdens of the Egyptians. And I will bring you unto the land concerning which I lifted up my hand to give it to Abraham, to Isaac, and to Jacob, and I will give it to you for an heritage, I am the Lord." Rashi solves several difficulties of this passage in his way, especially the one regarding the name JHVH.

Here it seems to be implied that this name was not known to the Patriarchs, whilst we find it in Genesis in God's revelations to them. Rashi explains that the name of four letters indicates the absolute truth vested in God, and the certainty of God making good his divine promises. Rashi supports this theory inductively by Biblical passages, in which that name occurs in this sense, especially when the formula, "I am JHVH," is added either to promises or to threats. Here we have also the introductory phrase, "I am JHVH," and Rashi explains it thus: "I have made the Patriarchs many promises which I prefaced with the words, 'I am God Almighty,' but they have never experienced the fulfilment of my promises; or, in other words, my name JHVH has not become known unto them." Rashi supports this further by observing that it is not said here: "I have not communicated that same unto them," but in the passive: "my name has not become known unto them." The verse, "I have established my covenant with them," is explained by Rashi: "I have said to Abraham, I am God Almighty . . . and I shall give thee and thy seed after thee the land of thy sojournings . . ." To Isaac: "I shall give thee and thy seed all these lands, and I shall establish the oath which I have sworn to thy father Abraham; an oath which was sworn with the words—'I am God Almighty.'" To Jacob: "I am God Almighty, be fruitful and multiply . . . and the

land which I gave to Abraham and Isaac I shall give
to thee, and to thy seed after thee I shall give the
land." "And I heard the groaning of the children
of Israel, I am JHVH, namely, in the slavery foretold
in the covenant between the pieces ; and I remember
that covenant. Therefore tell the children of Israel
I am JHVH, He in whom the truthful fulfilment of
promises is vested, the promises which he made to
the Patriarchs as God Almighty." Rashi then quotes
in support of his interpretation a verse, referred to
by R. Baruch b. R. Eliezer, from Jeremiah xvi. :
"Therefore I will cause them to know my hand and
my might, and they shall know that my name is
JHVH." Thus God indicates the fulfilment of His
threats by that name ; and how much more so the
fulfilment of His promises. Rashi proceeds : "Our
Sages explain the passage as follows : They say that
it is meant to be a rebuke to Moses, who had com-
plained to God (v. 22), saying : 'Lord, wherefore
hast thou evil entreated this people' : God, in His
mentioning the Fathers, said : Woe ! For those that
are lost and have not been replaced ! It is a mis-
fortune that the Fathers are dead ! Many a time
have I appeared to them as God Almighty, and they
said not, what is Thy name ? as thou hast asked :
What is Thy name ? I have established my covenant
with them, to give them the land ; and yet, when
Abraham wished to bury Sarah, he could not do so
till he had bought a grave at great cost ; and Isaac,

when he digged wells, the Philistines murmured ; and Jacob had to buy a portion of the field to pitch his tent. In spite of my promises they bore all this without making any reflections, and thou hast said : Wherefore hast thou evil entreated this people." But, Rashi proceeds, "this Midrash is not in harmony with the text, for several reasons : first, it is not said here about the Fathers : and my name JHVH they did not ask me for ; secondly, it cannot be said that the Fathers did not know that this was His name, for when God revealed Himself to Abraham at the covenant between the pieces, He said : 'I am JHVH who brought thee out from Ur Chasdim'; thirdly, how can the sequence of the sentences be understood in accordance with this Midrash. 'I have heard the groanings of the children of Israel— therefore tell them I am JHVH'? For these reasons I say, let the text be expounded according to its natural meaning, and so that everything runs according to the context, and let the Midrash stand also, for, as Jeremiah said : 'Is not thus my word like fire, says the Lord, and like the hammer which scatters the rock ; as the rock is scattered into many fragments, so the Torah bears many modes of interpretation.'" We must bear in mind that the interpretation which Rashi refuses to adopt here occurs in the Talmud, in the treatise of Sanhedim ; in the Midrash Tanchuma; and in the Midrash Rabba. Rashi, in his valuation of such interpretations, does no more than record certain homilectic observations laid down in the Talmud; but for himself he has selected his method and adheres to it.

In his pursuit of Pshat, Rashi pays, of course, great attention to grammar. It seems that, of the grammatical researches of his predecessors, only those of Menahem and Dunash were accessible to him, although he sometimes cites Sandiah with great respect. But he is by no means their slavish follower. He frequently disputes their derivations, and discusses his grammatical points with great acumen. Of the host of super-commentaries on Rashi, that by R. Isaac Auerbach, entitled Beër Rechobot, deals very lucidly with Rashi's grammatical notes on the Pentateuch. Nowadays, Rashi's grammatical points are looked down upon, but not always with justice; but it is true that, as far as we can ascertain, the researches of men like Ibn Ganach and others were unknown to him. Many modern scholars do not deign to go to Rashi for information. Gesenius said that he was no more than a traditional and Talmudic exegete, and occupied a place much below Ibn Ganach. For all that, there are instances that even Gesenius would have done well to consult Rashi. To give an example. On the word מלצר, in the first chapter of Daniel, Gesenius said that the usual way of taking this word as a proper noun, Hamelzar, was an error, but that the word means " cellar master "; if he had consulted Rashi he would have found that explanation there.

Were it possible to do so within the compass of a lecture, it would here be the place to cast a glance upon the translations of several of Rashi's works into Latin, made by Christians, and upon the use made by some Christian writers of Rashi in their own works. One instance must suffice. Nicholas de Lira was a voluminous commentator of the Bible ; the folios containing his writings are of a forbidding size. And what did the great Johann Renchlin say about him ? He was of opinion that if you took away out of Nicholas de Lira's books all that which he had taken from Rashi, not much would be left. In Reuchlin's own words : " Und wann die wörter und Reden, des Rabbi Salomonis, der uber die bibel geschrieben hat, uss unserm Nickola de Lyra, der auch uber die bibel geschrieben hat, cantzellirt und ausgethan werden, so wolt ich das uberig, so derselbe Nicolas de Lyra aus seinem eygen haupt uber die bibel gemacht hatte, gar in wenig bletter comprehendiern und begreiffen."

There are many points which can here only be indicated, but which deserve an exhaustive discussion : the Talmudical and Rabbinical writers, in the widest sense of the word, and the other authorities on which Rashi based his exegesis ; his predecessors and teachers ; his associates and disciples, some of whom, in a manner, collaborated with him ; the

Targumim, in as far as they were available by him,—for it seems that he did not know the so-called Targum of Jonathan to the Pentateuch. A comparison would be required between biblical exegesis, as exercised by the Spanish school, and that of the French school founded by Rashi. Abraham Geiger, whose sympathies did not naturally incline towards the Halachic and Midrashic exposition of the Bible, is yet constrained to assign, on the whole, the superiority to Rashi and his followers. He is of opinion that Bible exegesis does not always gain by enlightenment and expansion of view ; that the views are forced upon the Bible by twistings and contortions. He says that the school founded by Rashi was superior to the Spanish school in profound investigation of the spirit of the language, in a clear grasp of the detailed contents of a book, and in a general and critical insight in the ideas and conceptions of antiquity.

Besides the Pentateuch, Rashi wrote commentaries on the other books of the Bible, with the exception of the books of Chronicles and some verses of the book of Job. But the greatest attention of the scholars and critics has all along been particularly directed towards the Pentateuch. This is, above all, the case in reference to the history of Rashi's text in his commentary on that book. It goes without saying, that in the course of time inaccuracies and interpolations had slipped in, and additions belong-

ing to his followers inserted as if they were his.
The late Dr. Berliner spent many years in attempting
to give us an authentic and accurate text, by researches in all directions, and by collating a number
of manuscripts, and gave us the results of his labours
in notes to two editions, each of which one is a
complement to the other.   It is a matter of secondary
moment to consider those parts of the Talmud on
which Rashi has been erroneously held to have
written, or whether the commentaries on the Mishnah
of Aboth, and on Bereshith Rabba, which bear his
name, were really written by him.

But, in considering Rashi as an exegete, it is of the
greatest moment to take note of his Commentary on
the Talmud.   It is a gigantic work, and only a gigantic
mind like that of Rashi could have conceived
it.   And how are we to account for the striking
difference in method and execution between his
commentaries of the Bible and those of the Talmud ?
In the former he produces Agadic explanations, as
long as they harmonise with the text, but there is no
harmonising in his explanations of the Talmud.   In
the former his mode of expression is concise and
economical, but it may be called diffuse and verbose
when compared with his brief and laconic notes on
the Talmud.   He takes the Talmud exactly as it
stands ; he intends it to be understood apart from
all indirect considerations or preconceived notions.
He never allegorises, he never tries to explain any-

M

thing away. He never wants to soften harsh expressions; on the contrary, if they are harsh, he, as the faithful exegete, is at pains to bring the harshness out and make it understood. If there are passages which appear to others crude, and which they therefore want to explain away, by allegorising, by symbolising, or by other means, Rashi is unconcerned, and only wishes to make his readers understand what his text implies. He guides them in the intricacies of Talmudic dialectics, and with a few strokes and in the fewest of words unravels the most tangled skein of argumentation. With Rashi for a guide enigmatical sayings become clear, and with one word he forestalls questions which even the Tosafists sometimes spend pages to answer. Besides this, he was the great critic of the text of the Talmud. Our Talmuds present us essentially with Rashi's text. For Rashi lived a long time before printing was invented. Every letter in every single copy had to be separately produced by hand. Parchment, which was the principal writing material of the time, was very expensive. Whatever money the Jews had available for procuring the costly sheets was in the first instance expended on writing the scrolls of the Torah, or on prayer books. The copyist had to make a living out of his art of transcribing; and, however low the remuneration, the cost of preparing a copy of the Talmud must have mounted up to a considerable sum. Imagine only the labour and the expense of transcribing the whole of the Talmud! Roger Bacon, who lived over a century after Rashi, enumerates the obstacles he had to surmount when he wanted a copy of a book prepared. "How many parchments," he says, "and how many copyists were required, and how many proof copies had to be prepared, before one copy could be produced in a finished form to stand the final test! Many assistants were wanted, the merely mechanical work had to be entrusted to a number of lads, and many readers must be employed to purge the text from errors; inspectors were needed to prevent the copyists from committing frauds, and to superintend and account for the expenses." We may assume that only in a few cases copies of the Talmud were manufactured in such well regulated copying establishments. In most cases the eager and pious students procured copies in the best way they could, which means in the worst possible way. One inaccurate copy became the text from which to procure a still more corrupted copy. Marginal notes, extracts from the Halachoth Gedoloth, and other ancient works, were embodied in the text. And it was copies of such character which Rashi undertook to expound and correct. It is true Rashi's predecessors had already done good work in that direction; it appears that a *Perush* existed which had acquired authority on all sides. But after Rashi's efforts all such previous attempts became superseded. It became an absolute impossibility to study the Talmud without Rashi. His became the *Konteros*, the commentary *par excellence*. Never before nor after has a commentary of this character been written to any book. Rashi's corrections are almost all taken up in our copies, so that the readings which Rashi rejected are for the most part lost; a circumstance which is deplored by some as a loss to the historical critique of the Talmudic text, and which is only partly remedied by the newly discovered manuscript in Munich, which has been collated by Rabbinowicz.

How is it then that Rashi, who, in his commentaries on the Bible, intermingled pure exegesis with indirect hermeneutics to such a great extent, was, in regard to the Talmud, the sober dragoman who wished for nothing more than the clear understanding of the text? The ground is this, that both in the Bible and in the Talmud Rashi represented that which stamps the Jew with its individuality. In the Bible he had to find how Jewish life has to be evolved out of the written document; he had to introduce that which I call the living commentary of ages, and show its identity with the text of the Bible. But the Talmud, both in its Halachic and its Agadic parts, mirrors the life of the Jew in all its phases; it is itself that living commentary which had accompanied the Jews in all their wanderings from times immemorial, and of that living commentary Rashi was the faithful super-commentator.

Rashi was the great interpreter, and in his commentaries shows himself to have been an historical critic of the highest order. To give an instance : the vexed question of the origin, the authorship, the ancient and the present forms of the Sifra, the Sifre, the Mechilta, has exercised the acumen of profound scholars, and I think that the results arrived at by Friedman in his introduction to the Mechilta approach very near to the true solution. And what do we find there ? That the researches of modern learning on this subject coincide with the views of Rashi, although expressed by him only in occasional remarks, scattered here and there in his commentaries. Zachariah Frankel, in his valuation of Rashi's achievements in this direction, says, in reference to a certain point, that Rashi, who dives down deep and penetrates to the very centre of the earth, had here also taken the right view. We need not take notice of any of the legends with which piety has sought to glorify his memory. What difference does it make whether or no there is any truth in some of the miracles recorded about him ; whether or no he understood Persian, Arabic, Greek, Latin and German, whether or no he had studied astronomy, medicine, and other sciences ? He had a knowledge of the Bible in its minutest details, both to the letter and the spirit. He was at home in all the highways and by-ways of the Talmud. He was intimately acquainted with all that had become accessible to him of the Targumim, the works of the Geonim, the ancient Rabbinical writings, and the grammarians. He brought upon his exegetical efforts mental powers to bear that are not easily surpassed; he was pervaded with noble sympathies, which always made him forgetful of self and mindful of the intellectual needs of others; he mirrors in his commentaries all that had come down to him of the most elevated sides of Jewish life, which his exegesis reproduced. We are told that in advanced age he declared that if he were not too old he would write other commentaries, more strictly in accordance with Pshat pure and simple. It is idle to speculate on the aspect such commentaries might have presented. We may doubt whether they would have been the same reflex of comprehensive Jewish life and thought as those which we possess from his hand. It is the latter feature by which his exegesis has entered into Jewish life and has become part of its existence. Thus have the commentaries of the פושנדרתא, the Exegete of the Law, lived with us for eight hundred years, and will continue to live with us and to inspire us with religious life.

PUBLIC DISPUTATIONS IN SPAIN

THE tale of Jewish suffering since the exile furnishes monotonous reading to the callous, and heartrending reading to the humane. Flashes of light have occasionally broken through the gloom, at certain times, in certain localities. These were hailed by Jewish optimism as the harbingers of happier times, and magnified into legitimate grounds for triumph and rejoicing. But soon the sky was again overcast; persecutions were once more the order of the day, whether they be on a large or small scale, resulting in massacre and expulsion, or in petty, malicious and annoying molestations.

This preponderance of darkness over light, of evil over good, arises only from the environments in which the Jew is destined to move. But there is another aspect of our history in which the light dispels the gloom, in which the good is real, essential, enduring; to which the bad, however deplorable, bears only a slight proportion.

This is the aspect of our faith and race observable from within ; of the volume of capacity which the body Jewish has produced all along. There we see superior gifts of head and heart, moral and religious intensity reaching unsurpassable heights, purity, love and self-sacrifice of the highest order.

On the other hand, it cannot be denied that the same body Jewish has had much to suffer from malignant growths; that it occasionally developed venomous sores; which, it is true, never succeeded in penetrating to the core, yet were often instrumental in attracting the injurious miasms which constantly threatened us from without. In every generation some men appeared, who had broken loose from the community of Israel, thrown off their faith, and adopted that of the people that surrounded them. Having divested themselves of allegiance to their race and their religious inheritance, and having been spurred on by covetousness, ambition, and renegade zeal, joined their new brethren, not only in subscribing to their doctrines, but also in the baiting and persecution of their former co-religionists. More than that, they not only assisted them in their cruel designs, but instigated them to fresh attempts and aided them in their efforts. In these nefarious devices they had an advantage over their fellow torturers. They possessed a more or less intimate acquaintance with the literature of the Jews, with their rites and usages, which, however limited in some cases, surpassed that of those, who considered it a meritorious work to harass the Jews, and to try to exterminate them, or, at any rate, their religious convictions. "Your religion or your lives," was the challenge thrown at the Jews, at whole communities of Jews, at Jews of entire countries; thrown at them

with the flashing sword, with the flaming stake, or—
with what was in many cases not less of a death-
warrant — with wholesale expulsions. What a
nauseous notoriety did such perverts secure for
themselves throughout the ages ! Their real or
supposed superior knowledge of things Jewish was
eagerly sought and exploited by our enemies, in
order to frame charges by twisting and distorting
certain passages in our books. But it was not always
necessary to call in the help of the renegades ; the
latter offered themselves frequently of their own free
will. There is an old Jewish parable about the trees
supplying the handles for the axes with which they
were themselves to be felled ; these perverts turned
themselves into handles and axes at the same
time.

All means were considered justified to the end of
coverting us to Christianity. Degrading restrictions,
expulsion, steel, fire, have been the threats held out
to the recalcitrant Jews, and have been often unmercifully put into action. But the wolves were
not averse to donning sometimes the fleece of the
lamb. They tried to gain the Jews over by
persuasion. It was not the wily, kid-glove sort of
persuasion which we see employed at the present
day in the form of tea-meetings, medical assistance,
and other kinds of sly trickery, at which work, not
less than in the Middle Ages, pervert Jews are
found to lend a helping hand. Persuasion at the

time we have in view took the form of public disputations, which the Jews were summoned to
attend, to reply to charges levelled against them,
against their writings, and against their convictions.
The alternative ostensibly offered was : either convince us that we are wrong, or turn Christians. The
Jews knew full well that another alternative loomed
behind, to wit : either submit, or be prepared for
the direst persecutions of yourselves and all your
co-religionists.

And the method of persuasion by means of
public disputations was on a par with the tendency
that called them forth. Not for nothing does the
Amidah for the New Year and the Day of Atone-
ment contain the prayer : " Grant opening of the
mouth to those who abide in Thee." The Jews
were browbeaten, insulted, threatened at every
turn. Prominent in the insolent treatment of the
Jews was the hardened effrontery of the renegades,
who had indirectly instituted the disputations, and
now improved the opportunity of flaunting their
parvenu zeal for their new religion. Thus, there
were three principal levers at work to make
disputations a source of pain and peril to the Jews.
First, there were the Christian prelates and poten-
tates, to whom the conversion and torture of the
Jews were of paramount importance ; secondly, the
perverts, who joined them ; and, thirdly, the
helplessness of the Jews, who were unable to avert

the terrible consequences that hung over their heads and over those of their brethren in faith.

Spain was not the first country where public disputations had been forced upon the Jews. We need only remember the disputation in France, which had such fatal consequences, including the public burning of wagon loads of the most cherished Jewish books. The first disputation held in Spain was that in which one of the great luminaries, who have shed such brightness upon the gloom of the exile, stood on the defence against the attacks of the friar, Pablo Christiani.

Amidst the tale of so much sadness it is a solemn pleasure to refer to one of those men whose existence outbalanced a number of calamities and rendered them worth submitting to.

Moses ben Nachman, called by his fellow countrymen Bonastruc de Portas, quoted by the Jews by the initials of his name as Ramban, and known in literature as Nachmanides, was born in Gerona in 1195. It is not easy to describe the contents of a mind of a man like Nachmanides; it is difficult to sketch the superior powers of his intellect; it is more difficult to estimate the elevated qualities of his heart; and most difficult to comprehend the nature of a soul in which all these endowments were united and formed a harmonious whole. His religious convictions were based upon all that Jewish tradition offered, and this guided him in his religious and humanitarian acts. His disposition was kind and gentle, the purity of his heart can only be indicated negatively ; all impurity was far from him. He was wise, he was learned, he was always active for the good of his brethren.

He had mastered the Bible, the Talmud, and the Rabbinical writings. This, in the case of Nachmanides, means that he was a master in these disciplines and had gained an independent judgment all along their highways and byways. At the age of fifteen he commenced writing supplements to the religious code of R. Isaac Alfasi. Not long after he wrote a defence of that master, under the title of "The Wars of the Lord," against the critique of the eminent Talmudic scholar, R. Zerahya Halevi.

From these beginnings he proceeded to compose commentaries upon a number of Talmudical treatises, and wrote on several topics connected with the religious duties of the Jews. He always shows himself the clear thinker, the acute controversialist, and withal the man of feeling. The spiritual motives underlying the religious precepts made the tender fibres of his heart vibrate in sympathy. His mystical theories about the power of the soul to mould the body, and about retribution after death, breathe the tenderness of his feelings for the living.

Nachmanides was a philosopher. This has been denied by some writers. The truth is, he was not a harmoniser. He did not attempt to reconcile incongruous tenets from without with the contents of Judaism. He took Judaism as a phenomenon, investigated all it offered, in order to discover what it contained. He was averse to reading *a priori* notions into it; he clung to a method, pronounced to be the correct one by modern science. The eternal questions which obtrude themselves upon the thinking mind agitated him also to the full. He endeavoured to evolve answers to them from the Torah; and in his ardent piety, which prompted him to search for the divine, he was induced to adopt mystical points of view which appealed to him, rather than the enforced harmonisation of an one-sided intellectuality which leaves the heart cold and the religious cravings unsatisfied. Some writers speak of his inconsistency, because they miss the psychological moment which pervaded his speculations.

He held a prominent position amongst his brethren, who recognised his merits. He was Rabbi, first in Gerona, and afterwards in Barcelona. This was a position of honour, not of profit. A salaried Rabbi was unknown in those days, and it was only two hundred years after Nachmanides, that one of his descendants, R. Simon Duran, accepted emoluments for that position; and how pathetically does he recount the circumstances that had driven him to do so. Nachmanides was a physician, and probably made his living by his profession.

Now let us cast a glance upon the person who had the effrontery to join issue with him. He was an apostate Jew, who had assumed the name of Pablo Christiani, and had entered the order of the Dominicans. He used to travel backwards and forwards in his attempt to pervert the Jews, endeavouring to prove Christianity from Bible and Talmud. He was supported by the General of his order, Raymundus de Peñaforte. The latter had made it the object of his life to establish papal supremacy, and to torture Jews and Mahommedans into Christianity. For this purpose he founded seminaries for the study of Hebrew and Arabic, a mode of proceeding resoretd to by that class of Christianisers up to the present day. He was the spiritual director of Jayme, King of Aragon, who was submissive to Raymundus ; and no wonder, for he was sorely in need of the indulgences of his confessor. Jayme willingly supported the proselytisng measures of Raymundus. Here we have the three personages requisite to enact the drama of such disputations : the ruler of the country dependent upon the Church, the zealous and unscrupulous prelate, and the renegade Jew.

Raymundus contrived to institute a public disputation, at the Court of the king, between Moses ben Nachman and the friar Pablo, or Paul, Christiani.

Nachmanides was summoned to be the respondent
to the arguments which Pablo was to bring forward.
Pablo had assured the king that he would be able
to prove the Messianic claims for Jesus from
Talmud and Midrash. Nachmanides was permitted
to make some stipulations regarding the course of
the debate. It was the latter's object that an agenda
should be clearly enunciated, and that the disputants
should not swerve from the points submitted for
discussion. The points were : first, whether the
Messiah had already appeared ; secondly, whether
the Messiah, as foreshadowed by the prophets, was
to be a divine king or a man born of human parents ;
and, thirdly, whether the Jews or the Christians
possessed the true faith. Nachmanides further
demanded complete freedom of speech. The king
accepted the terms, but Raymundus wished to
qualify them by the proviso, that the freedom of
speech should not be abused so as to lead to
blasphemous remarks against Christianity. Nachmanides replied that he was fully well acquainted
with the rules of courtesy. Raymundus, evidently,
did not evince the same concern lest blasphemies
be uttered against the Jewish religion.

The disputation opened at Barcelona on the 20th
of July, 1263, in the king's palace, in the presence
of the whole court. The attendance included a
number of clericals, nobles and others, and, of
course, many Jews had to be present. The disputa-

tion lasted four days (non-consecutive). After the
third sitting a wish was expressed in several quarters
to terminate the discussion. The Jews of Barcelona
entreated Nachmanides to discontinue the debate
for fear of the Dominicans. A Franciscan monk,
Fray de Genova, joined them for reasons of his
own. The Christians of Barcelona desired the
same. Nachmanides communicated this general
wish to the king, but the latter ordered the
disputation to proceed.

The course of the discussion showed how badly
Pablo was equipped for crossing swords with
Nachmanides. His whole armament consisted in
some Agadic passages of no weight. He argued
that the Talmud implied that the Messiah had
already come, for there was an Agadic saying that
the Messiah was born on the day when the temple
of Jerusalem was destroyed. Nachmanides replied,
that, in the first place, he did not attribute any
authority to that Agada; and, secondly, if the information were correct it would prove the contrary
of that which Pablo wanted to deduce from it.
Pablo thought that his opponent had given him an
opening. "Behold," he exclaimed, "how this man
himself denies the authority of Jewish tradition."
Nachmanides proceeded, that this Agada either
contained an untrue statement or it bore an interpretation, symbolical or allegorical, which would
render it acceptable. But when taken in its crude,

literal sense, it contained a proof against Pablo's assumption. If Jesus was born on the day when the temple was destroyed he could not be the Messiah, for he was born and died before the temple was destroyed. According to Christian chronology, he was born seventy-three years before that event ; but, according to Jewish tradition, which gives the correct date, he was born two hundred years before the destruction.

Let us here make a brief digression in reference to the Talmudic statement about the time when Jesus lived, and which Nachmanides accepts as correct. According to the Talmud, Jesus lived at the time of R. Joshua ben Perachya. This statement is set aside by all modern historians, who either busy themselves with suggestions as to how the error may have arisen, or simply sneer at it. I will not enter upon a consideration of the question itself, but only wish to point out that the matter has been taken up in our days by George R. S. Meade, in a book entitled : *Did Jesus Live* 100 B.C. ? In that work the Talmudic statement, as all other statements on the subject, is considered from all points of view. It will suffice here to draw the attention of all who are interested in the question to that remarkable book. Only two sentences may be quoted here. The author says : ". . . that there was no scholar of repute nowadays who accepted the A.D. of Dionysius (Exiguus, who lived in the

N

sixth century) as coincident with the first year of the life of Jesus." And the author's concluding remark ran thus : " For my own part I feel at present somewhat without an absolutely authoritative negative to the very strange question : Did Jesus live 100 B.C. ?—and shall continue to feel so until all sides of the question have been again rigorously scrutinised by the ever finer critical equipment which the twentieth century must inevitably develop, and in the light of the great toleration which the ever-growing humanism of our day is extending to the most intractable questions of theology."

The point raised by Pablo as to the alleged proof of Christianity contained in the Talmud, is met by Nachmanides as follows : " It is," he says, "well known that all the incidents related about Jesus, about his birth and his death, would fall within the period of the second temple. The Talmudic Sages lived after the destruction of the temple. Now, suppose it were true that they believed in the Messianic character of Jesus, that they believed in him and his religion, why then did they not adopt the latter, but, instead, remained adherents of the Jewish faith and persisted in practising its observances ?

As to Nachmanides's belief in the authoritative value of Agadic statements—a point on which Pablo thought he had scored against him—he explained that our books were to be divided into three classes. First, there was the Bible, in which all of us believed

with perfect faith.   To the second class belonged the
Talmud, which contains the exposition of the precepts
of the Torah.   All the six hundred and thirteen
precepts of the Torah were explained in the Talmud,
and we believe in these explanations.   The third
class comprised the Midrash, which contains
sermones, homilies.   Our faith neither stands nor
falls with the belief or disbelief in their authority.
Against the Agadic passage under consideration,
other Sages averred that the Messiah would not be
born till the approach of the time for him to work
our deliverance from the dispersion.   Therefore, I
do not believe in this Agadic statement.

Omitting the various arguments propounded and
confuted during the disputations, the wrangles about
the true meaning of this or that biblical verse, it is
here only necessary to reproduce two or three
observations of Nachmanides.   He says : " The
question of the Messiah is not of that paramount
importance for our religion.   Thou, O King, art for
me of greater importance than the Messiah.   Thou
art a king, and he will be a king ; thou art a Gentile
king, and he will be a king of Israel ; for the Messiah
will be flesh and blood as thou art.   If I serve my
Creator now, permitted by thee to do so, in
exile, in affliction, in servitude, subject to general
scorn lavished upon me by all, my actions are
meritorious, and will meet with reward in the world
to come.   But when the king of Israel shall rule, I

shall perforce have to abide by the Jewish Torah, and my reward will not be so great."

"As for Jesus's alleged divine nature : Thou, a king, hast, as long as thou livest, heard priests, and Franciscans, and Dominicans, talk about his birth, and thy whole existence has become saturated with that belief. But it is opposed to reason, to nature. No prophet has ever said it ; neither Jews, nor any man can adopt it ; that the Creator of the Universe and all that is contained therein entered the body of a certain Jewess, there developed for several months, was brought forth into the world a human infant, grew up, and was handed over to his enemies, condemned to death, killed, and then, as you aver, lived, and returned to his original place."

" Isaiah prophesied that at the time of the Messiah, nation shall not lift sword against nation, they will no longer learn war. But ever since the birth of Christianity, up to the present day, the whole world is full of violence and devastation ; the Christians shed more blood than other peoples. How bad would it be for thee, O king, and for thy knights, were the art of war no longer learned."

These few quotations must suffice. Need it be said that the Dominicans spread the report that Nachmanides had been utterly worsted, and fled the city for shame ? The truth is, that Raymundus was far from being satisfied with the result of the disputation, and it was continued the next Saturday, in the synagogue of all places. After this, Nachmanides was received by the king, who dismissed him graciously and made him a present of a hundred maravedis.

But Raymundus did not acquiesce in the result. He induced the king to authorise Pablo to summon meetings for further disputations, and the Jews of Aragon were ordered to respond submissively to Pablo's call, whenever and wherever it may be, to meet his arguments, to supply him with the books he might require, and to pay the expenses of his crusade.

Finding his efforts to be of no avail, he determined to change his tactics. He had started with attempts to prove that the Talmud bore evidence to the truth of Christianity; now he accused the Talmud of containing blasphemous remarks against that religion. He laid his charges before the Pope Clement IV. This pope bore, before he was elevated to the papal throne, the name of Gui Legros, or Gui Foulques. As such he was appointed papal legate to the English court. He tried to interfere with the quarrels between Henry III and the Barons, but he met with insults from the latter which he never forgave or forgot. During his stay in England he became acquainted with some of Roger Bacon's aspirations, and this led to momentous results, into which it is here unecessary to enter. Nor can the consequences of Pablo's representations be

recorded here in detail. The gross outcome was
that the copies of the Talmud were confiscated, and
numerous passages, which the censors that were
appointed for the purpose considered to allude
adversely to Christianity, were expunged.

But this was not sufficient for the Dominicans ;
they desired to reach the person of Nachmanides
himself. The latter had composed a truthful and
sober report of the proceedings in Barcelona, copies
of which reached the Jews in several countries.
This came to the knowledge of the pope. He
upbraided King Jayme for harbouring such a person
in his land. The king was enjoined to dismiss all
Jewish officials and to punish Nachmanides. Where
would the venerable scholar, who was then over
seventy, turn for an asylum ? Whither does the
Jewish heart direct the footsteps of the Jewish
wanderer ? To the land of Israel, of course. It is
impossible here to enlarge upon his activities in
Palestine, upon his grief at the conditions prevailing there, upon the pathetic letters he directed
to his sons. He succeeded in collecting about him
a number of disciples, eager to listen to his teachings,
and it was in Jerusalem that he wrote his commentaries to the Bible. He died after having
carried on his blissful activity in the Holy Land for
more than three years.

I have dwelt upon the disputation at Barcelona
at too great a length, perhaps, chiefly because it was,

comparatively speaking, conducted in a rather gentle way; and was, in its consequences, however sad they were, milder than most of the subsequent ones.

The next disputation to be noted was that held at Valladolid, in 1336. The instigator was Abner of Burgos, a man of Jewish and of some secular learning, but of no principles. He was indifferent to religion, but was partial to a life of luxurious ease. His literary attempts in the fields of astrology and philosophy did not satisfy his desires. He was already advanced in years, when he was successful in improving his worldly position by turning Christian, and obtaining the post of sacristan at an important church at Valladolid. He explained his action by a theory which denied free will, and assumed the sway of inexorable necessity as ordained by the stars. He took the name of Alfonso, and was henceforth known as Alfonso Burgensis de Vallodolid. He made it the business of his remaining years to denounce the Jews in a number of writings, some of which evoked spirited rejoinders from Jewish scholars. A later writer referred to him, not as *Abner* (Father of Light) but as *Ab Choshech* (Father of Darkness). Besides these literary attempts, he raised an accusation against the Jews before Alfonso IX of Castile, reviving an old charge, as if the Jewish ritual contained a prayer, cursing the God of the Christians and his worshippers. The Jews of Valladolid denied the charge, and justly objected that the prayer did not allude at all to the Christians. But Abner Alfonso persisted, and prevailed with the king to summon the Jewish community to a public disputation. It took place in the presence of high officials and the Dominican clergy, and Alfonso had the satisfaction to obtain from the king an edict prohibiting the reciting of the incriminated prayer, under a penalty of one hundred maravedis.

The disputations held at Burgos and Avila must be recorded next. At that time the usurper, Henry II, occupied the throne of Castile, which he had wrested from his half-brother Pedro, after a series of sanguinary struggles. The Jews, whom Pedro had befriended throughout his reign, amply repaid his kindness by their staunch loyalty. They had joined his armies, fought bravely for him, and persisted in their fidelity to the last. During the vicissitudes of that struggle they had to endure indescribable sufferings at the hands of that horde of bloodthirsty cut-throats, called "the White Company," whose services Henry II made use of against Pedro. King Henry owed very much to the Church; the population also hated the Jews. Both these bodies demanded that the king should decree degrading and oppressive restrictions against the Jews. But Henry, in spite of the strenuous resistance the Jews had offered him before, was too much of a statesman to dispense with the services of such Jews as he could make use of. So he steered a

middle course, gave way to some of the demands of
Church and people, but refused to proceed against
the Jews in too drastic a manner. The concessions
included the right to compel the Jews to take part
in disputations ; and he empowered the apostate
Jews to arrange for them in whatever place in his
kingdom they might desire. One of them, Johann
of Valladolid, who had already before written against
the Jews, summoned them to a disputation, and it
took place at Burgos, in the presence of Gomez,
Archbishop of Toledo, and again in Avila, in 1375,
at which the whole of the Jewish community were
forced to repair to the church and attend the debate
in the presence of Christians and Mahommedans.
Rabbi Moses Hakkohen of Tordesillas was the
spokesman for the Jews. He had been bodily ill-
treated during the civil wars and robbed of all his
possessions. For four days this learned Rabbi had
to respond to the puerilities brought forward by
Johannes, which had for their object to find evidence
for all the Christian dogmas in the Hebrew scrip-
tures. The following may serve as a typical
example. The sixth verse of the ninth chapter of
Isaiah runs in the translation : " Of the increase of
the government and of peace there shall be no end,
upon the throne of David and upon his kingdom,"
etc. The Hebrew of the first phrase is, למרבה המשׂיה,
and masoretic tradition prescribes that the letter
מ (*m*) of למרבה, although in the middle of a word,

should have the form of ם (*m*) final. This exceptional form of the מ (*m*), says the apostate, points to Mary, and is clear evidence of the dogma of the virginity.

The debate terminated after four meetings. But then another apostate, a disciple of Alfonso of Burgos, challenged R. Moses to another disputation on Talmud and Agada, accompanied by the threat, in case of a refusal, he would denounce the Talmud to be an emporium of attacks upon Christianity. R. Moses had once more to undertake the repulsive task. He wrote a report of the debates, which he called "The Support of the Faith," and which he sent to the Jews of Toledo, to serve them as a guide in case they should be summoned to carry on a dispute. During these disputations R. Moses preserved a calm and composed demeanour, and never indulged in invective; for, as he wrote to his brethren in Toledo : "After all, the Christians wield the power, and are able to silence truth with their fists."

It is not worth while dwelling upon fictitious records of disputations, and of such which may be based upon fact but have not been historically authenticated. All the more attention must be given to the last of the public disputations in Spain ; the last, but the most deplorable of all.

The disputation at Tortosa presents a picture of unsurpassable anguish. It was preceded by suffering, it was followed by affliction, and was itself a crushing martyrdom. It was an event encased in harrowing torment. The monotony of it, the cruelty of it, the benumbing accumulation of woe ! Again we have the inexorable prelate, the unscrupulous renegade, the defenceless respondents, who trembled for their own fate and that of their unfortunate brethren. The disputation showed, moreover, a novel feature in the person of a maniacal preacher, whose portentous practices equalled his captivating eloquence and his unflagging zeal.

The prelate this time was no less a person than Pedro de Luna, afterwards Pope Benedict XIII; it is true, only one of the rival popes of the period, but who, for the time being, discharged the full papal functions in the countries which acknowledged his claims ; and who was powerful enough to let in a sea of troubles over the heads of the unfortunate Jews. When yet a Cardinal, he summoned Shem Tob ben Shaprut to a disputation, which took place in Pampeluna in the presence of priests and scholars. It induced Shem Tob to write a polemical work entitled *Aben Bochan* (Touchstone), for the purpose of providing his brethren with weapons of controversy, in view of the machinations of the apostates to call forth public disputations. It was Benedict who planned, with the assistance of his body-physician, the apostate Joshua Lorqui, the disputation at Tortosa. Benedict was playing for a great stake ;

a wholesale conversion of Jews, of the Rabbis and the masses, would have been a trump card in his gamble for the papal throne.

Joshuah Lorqui was one of the most dangerous specimens of his type. He had assumed the name of Geronimo de Santa Fe, Jerome of the holy faith, and evinced venomous malignity against his former brethren. He was well versed in Rabbinical lore, and was able to quote from the great commentators and exponents of Jewish law, such as Ibn Ezra, Rashi, Maimonides and Nachmanides. He was a master of sophistry, and of misconstruing and distorting casual Talmudical sayings of minor importance. Like several other enemies of the Jews, he paraded the Talmud at the same time as the judge on the bench and the felon in the dock. He undertook to prove that the Talmud contained clear evidence that the Messiah had already arrived in the person of Jesus, but, on the other hand, should the Jews prove obdurate, and refuse to embrace Christianity, a war to the death would be declared against the same Talmud, as being nothing but a sink of abomination and the principal cause of Jewish obstinacy. He composed a booklet (*Tractatus contra Judaeorum perfidiam*), containing nothing but vituperations, sophistries, and distortions of the simple meaning of innocent passages. Even such utter nonsense as the reference to the final ם (*m*) in the verse of Isaiah is repeated.

The nefarious influence of these enemies was equalled, perhaps surpassed, by the doings of the Dominican monk, Vincente Ferrer. In him zeal, sincerity, power of persuasion, went hand in hand with insane practices and implacable cruelty. He travelled far and wide to preach and exhort, and placed himself at the head of a band of flagellants. He and his followers went about unmercifully scourging their bare flesh, wandering in this manner from place to place, persuading others to do likewise, so as to work their salvation. Under such conditions he preached and electrified his hearers. He was indefatigable in his exertions to harass the Jews. He inveighed against the Maraños, those Jews who had outwardly adopted Christianity but who secretly practised Jewish rites. The fidelity of these people to their ancient faith, which the menace of terrible consequences had led them apparently to forsake, was so great, that the saying arose, that water could be wasted in three ways, by pouring it into the sea, by putting it into wine, and by using it for baptising a Jew. But he succeeded by threats and persuasion to induce many of the Maraños to make a penitent declaration of their new faith. He contrived, with the assistance of others, that laws were issued which not only made the life of the Jews well nigh unbearable, but also aimed at degrading all self-respect. He received permission to preach in the synagogues and to compel the Jews to attend. There he thundered at them, surrounded by armed soldiers and his maniacal horde of flagellants, with a cross in one hand, and a scroll of the Torah in the other. What direst persecutions had been unable to accomplish, sufferings, coupled with the spectacle of religious mania, partly succeeded in effecting. During Ferrer's activity numbers of Jews succumbed in many towns and accepted Christianity. Frenzy begets frenzy, and wholesale delirium is not less infectious than scarlet fever or small-pox.

The edict came forth, in 1412, that the most learned Rabbis and Jewish notabilities should repair to Tortosa for a disputation, in which Geronimo de Santa Fe would undertake to prove, from the Talmud, that the Messiah had already appeared in the person of Jesus. Non-compliance with the invitation was to be severely punished. The champions of Judaism thus summoned were one and all men of learning, of sincere religious fervour and nobility of character. They were penetrated by a sense of the dangers to themselves and their brethren, whatever the issue of the discussion might be ; or rather they were fully convinced that the discussion could only have one issue : the triumph of the sword over right, of the designs of the pope and the malevolence of the apostate over single-minded honesty.

It would be too much to give here the names of

all the respondents, or to enter upon the details of the debates, or upon the so-called arguments propounded. These particulars are given in the text-books that deal with the subject.

Two men were prominent among the defenders of the Jewish cause. Vidal ben Benvenisti ibn Labi and Joseph Albo. The disputation spread over a period of one year and three months—one year and three months of continuous torture. There were sixty-eight meetings—sixty-eight stages of acute agony. Although the respondents had agreed upon a united course of action, upon maintaining a calm demeanour, the racking nerve strain caused them frequently to yield to the impulse of the moment.

Nothing was neglected that could overawe the Jews. Before the commencement of the disputation they had to come before the pope to register their names ; he was gracious and affable, and promised them complete freedom of speech. The disputation started the following day. The pope was surrounded by cardinals and prelates, decked in their gorgeous vestments ; the audience numbered over a thousand. The pope opened the sitting with a speech, in which he pointed out that the question before them was not that of the truth of Christianity or Judaism, because Christianity was above dispute. It was merely a question whether the Talmud recognised Jesus as the Messiah. He was followed by Geronimo, whose speech was long-winded, replete with so-

phistical subtleties and fulsome flattery of the pope.
He threatened the Jews, applying to them the verse
of Isaiah : " If you consent and obey you will enjoy
the good of the land, but should you refuse and
disobey you will be devoured by the sword."

Vidal ben Benvenisti, who, on account of his
knowledge of Latin had been chosen by the Jews as
their principal spokesman, replied in that language ;
pointing out, *inter alia*, that they had been threatened
by Geronimo before a single argument *pro* or *contra*
had been uttered. This was met by the pope with
the remark that this was certainly wrong, but that
the misdemeanour must be accounted for by his
Jewish descent. The Jews requested the pope to
relieve them, on the ground that Geronimo based
his arguments on scholastic dialectics, whereas their
faith rested on tradition and not on syllogisms. It
is needless to say that the pope refused their request.

The disputation proceeded under the presidency
of the pope, until his own troubles necessitated his
frequent absence. The Jews had answers in plenty
to Geronimo's nonsensical sophistries, but their
words were twisted as soon as they were uttered.
They were incessantly being terrorised, and at length
the pope threatened them with death. Their resistance proving unbroken, their enemies turned on
to the other tack, namely, that of accusing the
Talmud of being a storehouse of iniquities of every
description ; Geronimo was assisted herein by other

apostates that were present. The Jews, of course, defended the incriminated passages.

We have seen that Vincente Ferrer and his savage hordes had succeeded in inducing a certain number of Jews to go over to Christianity. Groups of such were summoned to Tortosa, and they had to appear at the meetings, to make a declaration of their newly adopted Christian faith. But this form of intimidation was of no more avail than any other. Yet, a year and a quarter's heckling, bullying, threatening, and the sense of peril to themselves and to their oppressed brethren, was not without effect. It was more than flesh and blood and nerves could bear. The respondents longed for the end of the ordeal, and in order to effect this the majority of them signed a declaration that they did not attach any authority to the incriminated passages, and that they repudiated them. Of course, this concession was no concession at all; they had not been brought a step nearer to the adoption of Christianity. Their declaration, extorted by fifteen months of mental strain, left the question exactly where it had stood before. The staunchness of these respondents was not impaired, the opponents had not gained an inch of ground, and all the infernal machinery set in motion to turn them into Christians had failed. Besides, not all the respondents put their signature to that document. Vidal Benvenisti and Joseph Albo did not concede even this little. They declared their belief in the authority of the Talmudic Agada; only the passages in question must be properly understood, and must not be condemned on the strength of their literal meaning. In one word, the disputation at Tortosa was for the instigators an utter failure. The consequence was obvious. All the sluices of persecution and cruelty were thrown open, and the text-books of Jewish history have a dreadful tale to tell of sufferings which the discomfiture of the attempts to occasion a wholesale apostacy of the Jews had in its train.

There is one feature which runs like a red thread through all these disputations, in Spain as everywhere else. Whilst the Jews could only rest on their convictions, their opponents rested their arguments upon the sword. They felt themselves to be the powerful party, and knew not only how to use their power but also how to abuse it to the utmost. In every case the Jewish cause was lost, not by its weakness but by the power of the sword. The Gauls, after the battle on the banks of the Allia, had the Romans at their mercy. The latter had to buy the withdrawal of their foes for a large amount of gold. The legend tells us that, whilst the gold was being weighed out, the Romans suspected the correctness of the weights put in the scales, and when they protested, Brennus, the leader of the Gauls, placed his sword also in the scales. The Roman

Tribune asked him what he meant by this? Brennus answered : "This means *Vae Victis !* (Woe to the conquered !). This describes partly, but only partly, the mutual position of the Jews and those who challenged them to these disputations. The latter never failed to put the sword into the scales, and it meant Woe—Woe unspeakable, immeasurable, calculated to crush, to extirpate. But "Woe to the conquered"? No; who was conquered? Not the Jews. They were degraded, robbed, massacred, forced to wander not knowing whither. They had to go through the whole gamut of suffering. But they were not conquered. Albo, one of the heroic defendants of Tortosa, composed afterwards his philosophical work, *The Book of Principles*, in which he purposed to fix the fundamental bases of the Jewish religion. Philosopher, Talmudist, physician, he was fully equipped for the task. He was not prepared to follow obediently the footsteps of the Jewish philosophers who had preceded him. He examined their conclusions, and, instead of the thirteen principles of Maimonides, he assumed only three : God's existence, Revelation, and reward and punishment. Another champion at the same disputation, Vidal Benvenisti, wrote a defence of the Talmud against Geronimo's aspersions, under the title of *The Holy of Holies*. The polemical writings of this period deserve to form the subject of a special enquiry.

Neither were the Jews conquered, nor was the much maligned Talmud. That wonderful record, in which are deposited the thoughts, the feelings, the religious practices, civil and criminal legislation, moral lessons, religious lessons, traditions, narratives, parables, proverbs, and many more subjects; that compilation depicting the life of the Jews during a number of centuries, and regulating the life of the Jews for many centuries to come; that Talmud had been treated in the same way as the Jews. It has been calumniated, persecuted, publicly burned. Whole libraries of this, and other Jewish books, have been wantonly destroyed. What has been its fate in the end? The Talmud survives. In our own time edition follows edition. Taking the last hundred years, we find that, besides copies of separate treatises, the whole of the Babylonian Talmud has been printed during that period more than twenty-five times, which, taking that figure, would make an average of one edition for every four years.

The Talmud survives, so do the Jews. The persecutions, and the so-called disputations, have exterminated neither them nor their faith. And the words of Deuteronomy (iv. 4), which our little ones are taught to utter as soon as they are deemed capable of praying, remain unshaken: "You who cling to God, your God, you are alive, all of you, this very day."

PFEFFERKORNIANA

A BOOK was published in 1530, entitled : *Der gantz Jüdisch Glaub mit sampt einer gründlichen und wahrliaften Anzaygung aller Satzungen*, etc., by Anthonius Margaritha. The author was a converted Jew, one of those who applied the knowledge of matters Jewish, which they had acquired when young, to the belittling and contumely of their former co-religionists. The book contains some illustrations, which intend to depict some of the Jewish rites and ceremonies. Four of these attract our particular attention. They represent the blowing of the trumpet on New Year, the standing by the river on that day to recite the verses of Micah, chapter vii, 18-20 (Tashlich), the waving of fowls (Kappara), and the blessing of the people by the priests. The corners of each illustration are filled up with representations of other rites referring to the season of the year. Some of them were reproduced in the *Jewish Encyclopædia* and elsewhere. Thus, for instance, the bookseller Martin Bresslauer, in one of his artistically got up catalogues (No. 22) offered

for sale a copy of the extremely rare first
edition of Margaritha's book, and embellished
his notice with a reproduction of Margaritha's
woodcut of " Kappara." The same woodcut
appears also in the *Jewish Encyclopædia*, s.v.
" Kappara," which work also contains another s.v.
"Synagogue," and, I believe, also a third of
these illustrations, all taken from Margaritha's book
of 1530. The view of the *Jewish Encyclopædia*
is followed in the catalogue of *Judaica and
Hebraica* (No. 419), issued this year by Maggs
Brothers.

Harry Bresslau, in an article on Josel of Rosheim [1]
briefly mentions Professor Ludwig Geiger's reference
to the woodcuts, which appeared in the second edition
of Margaritha's book—the first edition not having
been accessible to Geiger—and says that those of
the second edition are reproductions of the illustrations in the first. Geiger's reference appears in the
second volume of the *Zeitschrift* (1888, p. 324).
Having given the title of Margaritha's book, he says
that the text contained some woodcuts representing
the blowing of the Shofar, Kappara, Tashlich, and
the blessing by the priests, and adds, that a
reproduction of one or two of them would prove
instructive for the history of Jewish usages.

We see that one and all ascribe the original

---

[1]. *Zeitschrift fur die Geschichte der Juden in Deutschland,*
edited by L. Geiger, V, 1892, p. 310, n. 2.

issue of these four illustrations to Margaritha, in whose book they made their first appearance in 1530. We need not be surprised at this. The book aroused great interest, and it was reprinted several times. Some of the later editions omitted the pictures, but the scholars interested in the subject turned to the earlier issues and saw no reason why they should not connect them with Margaritha.

The truth of the matter is that, as regards Margaritha, they are a plagiarism. He plagiarised them from Pfefferkorn's pamphlet, which appeared in 1508, in German : Ich heyss ein buechlyn der Juden Beicht, etc., and in Latin : *Libellus* de Judaeonum confessione, etc. A copy in high German, two in low German, and two Latin translations were printed in the same year. Professor Geiger's biography of Johann Reuchlin appeared in 1871, in which he observes in reference to the pamphlets (p. 212), that they all contained pictures ridiculing the Jewish rites. In the *Zeitschrift*, also he refers to Pfefferkorn's *Judenbeicht*, only two pages before mentioning Margaritha's woodcuts. Evidently, when writing in 1888, that which he had written in 1871 had slipped his memory. Such things will happen ; a writer is only human.

In order to enable the reader to judge for himself, a reproduction of the four woodcuts are given here,

THE BLOWING OF THE TRUMPET

TASHLICH

KAPPARA

THE PRIESTS BLESSING THE PEOPLE

taken from one of those extremely rare pamphlets of
1508. It is not necessary to give here a translation
of the scurrilous and frequently untrue comments of
Pfefferkorn. A glance will show the difference
between the originals and Margaritha's imitations.
The pictures in Pfefferkorn's booklet display some
skilful draughtsmanship; the figures are correct in
their outlines and show careful handling. Those
in Margaritha's book are the work of a bungler, and
are not only a caricature of Jewish ceremonies but
also of the pictures copied. Besides, the copies
were taken from the originals direct on the wood-
block from which they were printed in Margaritha's
book. The consequence is that those parts of the
pictures which appear in the originals of 1508 on the
right show in the copies of 1530 on the left, and
vice versa; rechte Hand linke Hand Alles vertauscht,
as the German doggerel has it.

In my article on Pfefferkorn,[1] I dwelt on some
efforts made to whitewash that pervert. I alluded
briefly to the attempts made by one, D. Reichling,[2] in
his defence of the notorious Ortvinus Gratius, one
of the principal aiders and abettors of Pfefferkorn in
his nefarious machinations against the Jews. It is
true, the ordeal Ortvinus Gratius had to undergo
through Reuchlin's less delicate champions was

---

1 See my "Book of Essays," pp. 73-115.

2 "Ortvinus Gratius, Sein Leben und Wirken," by Dr.
D. Reichling.

severe. He was the target at which the poisonous arrows were directed by Crotus Rubianus, Ulrich von Hutten, and their associates. The *Epistolae Obscurorum Virorum*, the letters of the Nobodies,[1] in which these protagonists of an excellent cause employed a very questionable method, were represented by their fictitious authors as having been directed to Ortvinus Gratius, and he was covered with ridicule and insults. Whether he was more guilty than the other Jew baiters of Cologne or not, it is certain that he was by no means the innocent, or even the sainted personage, as whom Reichling presents him to the public. But then Reichling writes as a special pleader ; he was a follower of Janssen. That learned author deals with the history of the German people from a staunch Roman Catholic standpoint. He consequently shifts, in his survey of the Reuchlin-Pfefferkorn episode, the blame for the virulent agitation from the shoulders of the Cologne crew to those of their opponents. As is usual in such cases, Reichling outdoes Janssen in his defence of the Cologne party. He refers to the Jews as a class of people sufficiently notorious, forgetting that the class of writers to which he belongs are themselves sufficiently notorious.

An example of Reichling's clap-trap argument is particularly manifest in his treatment of the case of

---

[1] This is the real meaning of the expression. See my " Book of Essays," p. 108. Mr. Griffin Stokes, *The Epistolae Obscurorum Virorum*, Introduction, p. xlv., has come to the same conclusion.

Petrus Ravennas. This Italian jurist had been received in Cologne with open arms. But the praise soon turned into hatred, and Jacob van Hoogstraten, soon after his appointment as Grand Inquisitor, won his first spurs in the persecution of that scholar. His crime was that he had given it as his opinion that the authorities of German States acted in opposition to natural and divine justice, nay, that they committed a deadly sin when they allowed the corpses of hanged persons to rot on the gallows. Reichling neither denies, nor does he defend, the practice itself ; he only maintains that, Ravennas being an alien, it was no business of his. Was it right for the alien immigrant to attack *German* institutions, and *German* usages, and to declare that those who practised them were doomed to eternal punishment ? The cogency of such a line of defence is obvious, although, unfortunately, it is by no means unusual in our time.

Professor Geiger frequently attempts to extenuate Pfefferkorn's machinations and those of his abettors, nor is he always fair in pointing out Reuchlin's delinquencies. The question at issue was whether the Jewish books contained matter antagonistic to Christianity or not. The Archbishop of Mayence received in 1510 a mandate to submit the question to the Universities of Cologne, Mayence, Erfurt and Heidelberg, to the Grand Inquisitor, Jacob van Hoogstraten, to Johann Reuchlin, and to other men acquainted with Hebrew literature and who were not Jews. Pfefferkorn was appointed the agent to transmit the reports to the Emperor.

Geiger correctly remarks (p. 236) that the reports of Hoogstraten and of the University of Cologne were identical in tendency. Excerpts from the Jewish books should be made for examination, and the advisability of burning the latter would become evident. What was to be the nature of that examination ? Geiger quotes Hoogstraten's words :
et institueretur contra Judaeos solemnis inquisitio, et super articulis- extractis mature examinarentur.
"A solemn *inquisitio* should be instituted against the Jews, and they should be heard and examined concerning these excerpts." The words are clear enough. They indicate that a tribunal of the inquisition should be instituted, before which the Jews should be called to answer for the suspected passages. This interpretation of the words which Grätz gives is undoubtedly correct. Surely *solemnis inquisitio* means an inquisitorial investigation, in the sense which the word *inquisitio* bore in those days, especially in a report of a Grand Inquisitor. Geiger, however, takes Grätz to task for imputing to the Grand Inquisitor a desire to institute an inquisitorial tribunal. He says that Hoogstraten merely demanded a measure, not at all inhuman, to inquire from the Jews what they meant by the incriminated passages ; just to have a little con-

fabulation, to ascertain how the Jews understood them. Geiger, in proof of his view, points out that in the report of the Cologne University, which essentially agrees with that of Hoogstraten, the words are : *vocentur publice Judaei et super his (articulis) audiantur et examinarentur.* The word *inquisitio* is not used, and Geiger is of opinion that these milder terms explain that Hoogstraten, with his brusque expression of *solemnis inquisitio*, meant nothing worse.

It is strange that Geiger (p.258) attaches to the identical term, *inquirere*, the meaning which it always has when coming from such a quarter. After Reuchlin's *Augenspiegel* (Spectacles) had appeared, it was submitted to Hoogstraten and some of his colleagues for adjudication, and Reuchlin was warned of the danger that threatened him from their decisions . . . *quidam, quia libellus combureretur, quidam, quia auctor inquireretur.* Some were for burning the booklet, others thought the author *inquireretur.* Here Geiger translates *inquireretur :* be examined under torture (peinlich befragt). But why should *inquirere* here mean : investigation under torture, and in the other passage : a cross-examination devoid of all unkind intention ? The Grand Inquisitor used the term in either passage, and the words of the Cologne University cannot explain away Hoogstraten's grim intentions. The reverse is the case. Hoogstraten's words throw light on the intentions of the Cologne University, "A thorough examination of the Jews about the suspected passages" in those days and from such a source ! Can there be any doubt about the meaning of such an expression ? The mildness of the terms deceived nobody. Such suave and sleek words covered the most severe measures among those tribunals. When a person was condemned to be burned alive, the words in which the sentence was couched were, "that he be delivered up to the secular authorities to deal with him in their mercy, and without the effusion of blood." In the case before us, all that can be said is, that Hoogstraten was more outspoken, and did not make use of the official hypocritical circumlocution.

Reuchlin printed, about 1512, the translation of an epistle of a certain Hippocrates "on the preparation of man" (*Hippocrates de praeparatione hominis ad Ptolemaeum regem*). He dedicated it to Johann Stoccarus, a physician of note, who became body physician to the Duke of Bavaria. Reuchlin mentions that the science of medicine was revealed by God to the angels ; these transmitted it to the Jews, from whom it came to the Greeks and Romans, and subsequently to the Germans. Geiger observes (p. 163) that Reuchlin could not suppress the remark ; that in saying this he did not desire to honour the Jews of his own time. The fact is, that Reuchlin only inveighed against those *baptised* Jews who

P

posed as medical men without possessing any knowledge whatever of the art.

"Do not imagine that I wish to impart honour to such Jews as allowed themselves to be baptised, or moistened, or immersed in water, either because they wanted to escape punishment for crimes committed, or to increase their income, or to indulge in their licentious desires. I would not apply to such vagabonds the honourable title of physician. You find many of them wicked beasts, devoid of all shame, posing as members of your body, or foisting themselves upon us as theologians and Hebraists, being in either case as ignorant as they are perfidious. Both you and I have had to suffer at the hands of a convert of that class, each of us was obliged to chastise one of that sort." Not a word is said here against the general body Jewish or their medical men.

Reuchlin was not devoid of numerous friends; some of them eagerly undertook his defence. One of them, Petrus Galatinus, wrote a voluminous work in dialogue form,[1] the assumed speakers being Reuchlin (under his Latinised name of "Capnio"), Galatinus, and Hoogstraten. His citations from the Talmud and other Hebrew books are for the most parts plagiarised from Porchetus and Raymundus

---

1 Opus christianae Reipublicae maxime utile de arcanis catholicae veritatis contra obstinatissimam Judaeorum nostrae tempestatis perfidiam, etc. Orthonae Maris, 1518

Martini. The book was printed by Hieronymus
(Gershon) Soncino, and is prefaced by some laudatory
verses in Hebrew.   Here is one of them reproduced,
mistakes and all, exactly as it appears in the
volume :—

זֶה הַסֵּפֶר נוֹתֵן שֶׁפֶר

סִתְרֵי תַּלְמוּד לְכָל פְּזַר

סוֹד מָשִׁיחַ בּוֹ יָשִׂיחַ

אָב בֶּן רוּחַ אֶחָד שׁוּנֵר

יַהֲרוֹס שְׁטוֹת הַגּוֹשְׁטַרְטוּס

גְּלַטִּינוּס אֱמֶת גָּזַר

הוּא כַּחוֹמוֹת אֶל הַחָכְמוֹת

אֶל תּוֹרַת אֶל בַּל יִקְרַב זַר

It requires some explanation how it is that
Gershon Soncino allowed such an eulogy of an anti-
Jewish book to be printed by him, not to speak of the
book itself. Steinschneider, in his catalogue of the
Hebrew books in the Bodleian library, quotes some
observations of Almanzi, who found some ambiguity
in one or two expressions, and thus suggests a
covert disapproval of the book. He says that the
word גזר, whilst meaning " he decides אמת the truth,"
bears also the meaning of " he cuts off the truth,"
and that חומת אל החכמות, "the walls of all wisdom,"

hints also ambiguously at the "obstacles against wisdom," so that it is precluded from singing in public, as required in Proverbs i. 20. Almanzi also thought to have discovered similar ambiguities in another of these eulogistic poems. However this may be, the above poem is nothing but an imitation of the laudatory poem prefacing the *editio princeps* of Ibn Tibbon's translation of R. Jehuda Halevi's Kuzari (1506).[1] The exact reproduction is :—

זֶה הַסֵּפֶר נוֹתֵן שֶׁפֶר
חֵן שֵׂכֶל טוֹב לְכָל פְּזַר

הוּא כְחוֹמוֹת אֶל הַחֲכמוֹת
אֶל תּוֹרַת אֶל בַּל יִקְרַב זָר

טַעֲנוֹת יַהֲרוֹם לַאֲפִיקוֹרוֹס
וּלְהָשִׁיב לוֹ אוֹמֶר גָּזַר

בּוֹ תּוּשִׁיּוֹת תּוֹרָנִיּוֹת
טַעֲנוֹת חֶבֶר אֶל הַכּוֹזַר

It seems that at the Soncino printing offices a number of poems of that kind were kept in stock, or, at least, that such a poem once used was preserved to be remodelled and used again as the occasion required. That such praise of Galatin and

1 See *Giacomo Manzoni, Annali tipografici dei Soncino*, III, 464.

his book was printed in Gershon Soncino's office
may be explained by the circumstance that the latter
had probably no inkling of its contents. His
printing establishments were spread over several
cities, and he could not, therefore, superintend
himself all the Hebrew, Greek and Italian
works produced by his firm. Add to this that
he probably knew no Latin, as Abraham Geiger
proved, the fact that prefatory poems of praise of
attacks upon Jews will not appear so strange after
all.

One more interesting incident in the life of
Reuchlin is worth noting. He was sent to Rome as
delegate by the elector Philip, Count Palatinate,
and, during his stay, made use of the opportunity to
further complete his knowledge of Hebrew. He
took daily lessons from R. Obadiah Sforno, who
was a physician by profession, and wrote commentaries to a number of books of the Bible, which
are frequently reprinted, even at the present time.
Reuchlin, who greatly appreciated Sforno's instruction, could not withhold the remark that his
teacher's fee was rather high (*non sine insignis
mercedis impendio*) ; and Melanchthon relates that
he had to pay a ducat for a lesson of an hour's
duration.[1]

This must have appeared to a German of that age

1. L. Geiger, *Das Studium der hebräischen Sprache in
Deutschland von Ende des 15 bis zur mitte des 16 Jahrhunderts*,
1870, p 39, n I.

a prodigious remuneration, some even must have thought it an outrageous imposition. So it would have been if it had been paid in Germany. But account must be taken of the difference between Germany and Italy. We might as well apply the standard of remuneration for professional services obtaining not so long ago in some small town of Germany or Russia to that of London or New York. What was the monetary value of learning and its advancement in Italy during, and for a long time after, the renascence of letters? Let us hear Macaulay's description, in his essay on Macchiavelli. "From this time, he says, the admiration of learning and genius became almost an idolatry among the people of Italy. Kings and republics, cardinals and doges, vied with each other in honouring and flattering Petrarch. . . . To collect books and antiques, to found professorships, to patronise men of learning, became almost universal fashion among the great. The spirit of literary research allied itself to that of commercial enterprise. Every place to which the merchant princes of Florence extended their gigantic traffic, from the bazaars of the Tigris to the monasteries of the Clyde, was ransacked for medals and manuscripts. Architecture, painting and sculpture were magnificently encouraged. Indeed, it would be difficult to name an Italian of eminence, during the period of which we speak, who, whatever may have been his general character, did not at least affect a love of letters and of the arts—knowledge and public prosperity continued to advance together. Both attained their meridian in the age of Lorenzo the Magnificent."

It was about the time when Lorenzo died that Reuchlin entered upon his embassy to Rome. He solicited instruction from a man of high position and considerable attainments. Sforno, used to the conditions in vogue in Italy, certainly must have charged an ambassador from a ruling prince a fee compatible both with the position of the teacher and the dignity of the pupil. Sforno would no doubt have been astonished at umbrage being taken by the Germans at the amount charged, in the same way as the fee was deemed extravagant in penurious and parsimonious Germany, which only just began to open its eyes to a culture which had already long ago found its home in Italy.

INDEX.

INVENTORY '80

DATE DUE